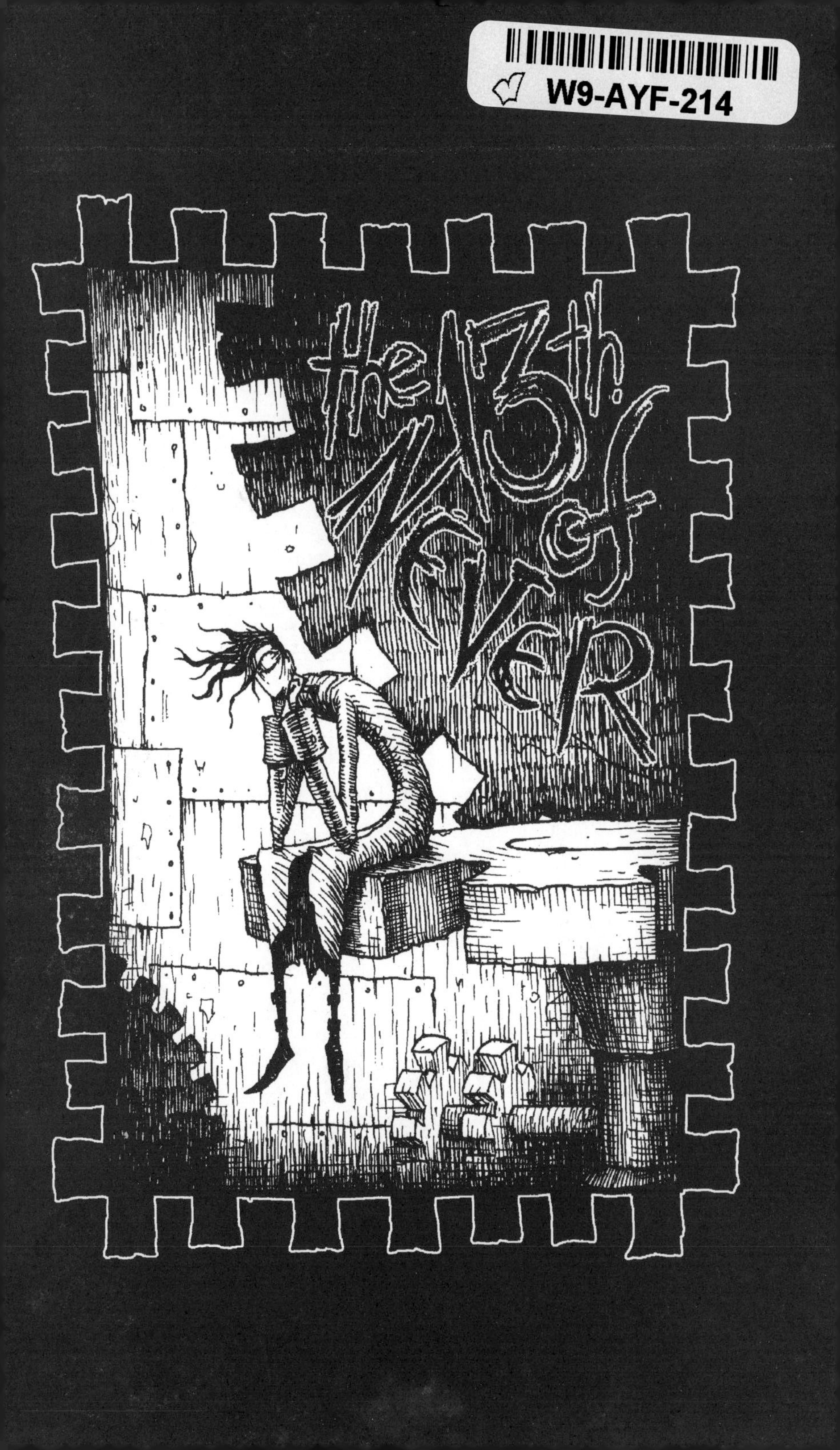
the 13th of Never

Zazil sat on his bed, staring into the blackness of his room. It was one a.m., Friday, October the 13th, the morning of his birthday, and he couldn't sleep. He could never sleep on the night of his birthday. The anticipation of what was to come made him uneasy every year.

In the distance, the rhythmic sounds of a train became steadily louder. Zazil often wondered where the noises came from. He never recalled seeing train tracks anywhere near his house, let alone a train. Like clockwork, the noises started the same time every night, and they seemed to last longer than train noises should.

Lulled by the ambient sounds of steam and metal, Zazil drifted off into the darkness of his own head....

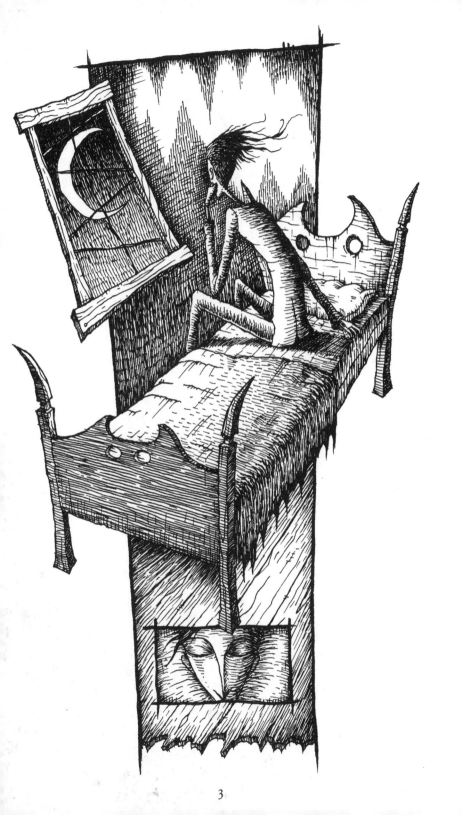

"Ouch!" cried Zazil. Every morning he awoke abruptly from his slumber to the crass sound of his alarm clock, causing him to bang his head on the bed board. He rubbed his sleep-encrusted eyes and scanned the four corners of his room. The many good luck charms and trinkets everywhere reminded him of what day it was. It was his birthday, which meant if he didn't want anything bad to happen, he would have to buy another good luck charm. His mother had done it for him ever since he could remember, with the exception of his 13th birthday. That was the day she died.

It was after his 13th birthday that Zazil realized how severe his perpetual bad luck really was, and his mother's death was proof. She didn't speak of it much other than on his birthdays, when she would give him a new charm. She just told him it was for his own protection against evil spirits and any other harm that he may encounter. What he didn't know was that the charms protected her from his bad luck as well. The charms prevented death, but some

4

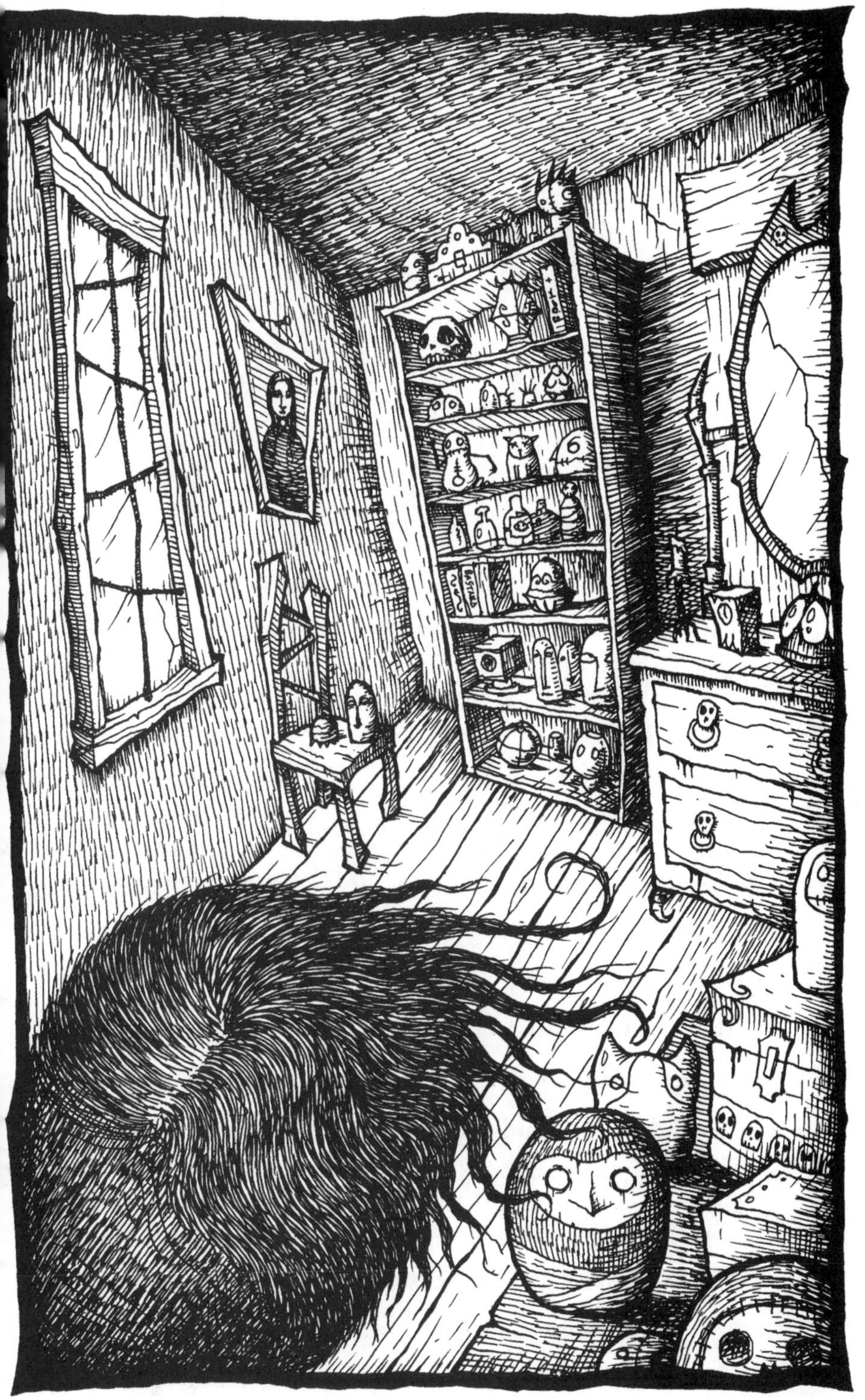
BASTARD

kind of misfortune occurred daily, no matter how small. A typical day for Zazil still included dropping, breaking and often losing important items while managing to somehow mangle, trip or hurt himself.

Zazil was an aberration of sorts, you see.... He was born on the 13th hour of the 13th day of October. This was not what made him strange, though. No, the fact that he was the 13th son of a 13th son made him a little different. You'd think that being the only one out of 13 children to not be stillborn would be a lucky thing. You'd think he'd be clairvoyant and full of magical powers. Nope. Instead he was cursed with wretched luck. He had always assumed that his father had abandoned him, but what no one knew is that he had died the day Zazil was born. Mysteriously, strangely, unknown.

The disaster that lay ahead was not totally unforeseen, though. No, there was one solitary warning that was completely ignored from a gypsy that Zazil's mother encountered on the way to the outdoor market. Why she chose to ignore it was uncertain. Perhaps she was still hanging on to the hope that after giving birth to twelve dead children this one would be all right. Whatever the case, had she listened to the gypsy, she and her husband might have still been alive.

"Dispose of the child if you want to live!" hissed the gypsy as she passed Zazil's pregnant mother on the cobblestone path. "He will bring pain and misfortune on us all if he is born!"

"I don't understand," replied Zazil's mother.

"His father is a 13th son and so shall your child be!" cackled the gypsy.

"Thank you for your concern, but you can't scare me with fairy stories," Zazil's mother answered, a bit worried.

"If you're not concerned about your own safety, at the least keep the rest of us safe from him. You must protect others from the little beast by giving him a good luck charm on every one of his birthdays," warned the gypsy. "He's not meant to be born, and you must take precautions." She then grabbed Zazil's mother's hand and placed a smooth, round charm carved of rock into her palm.

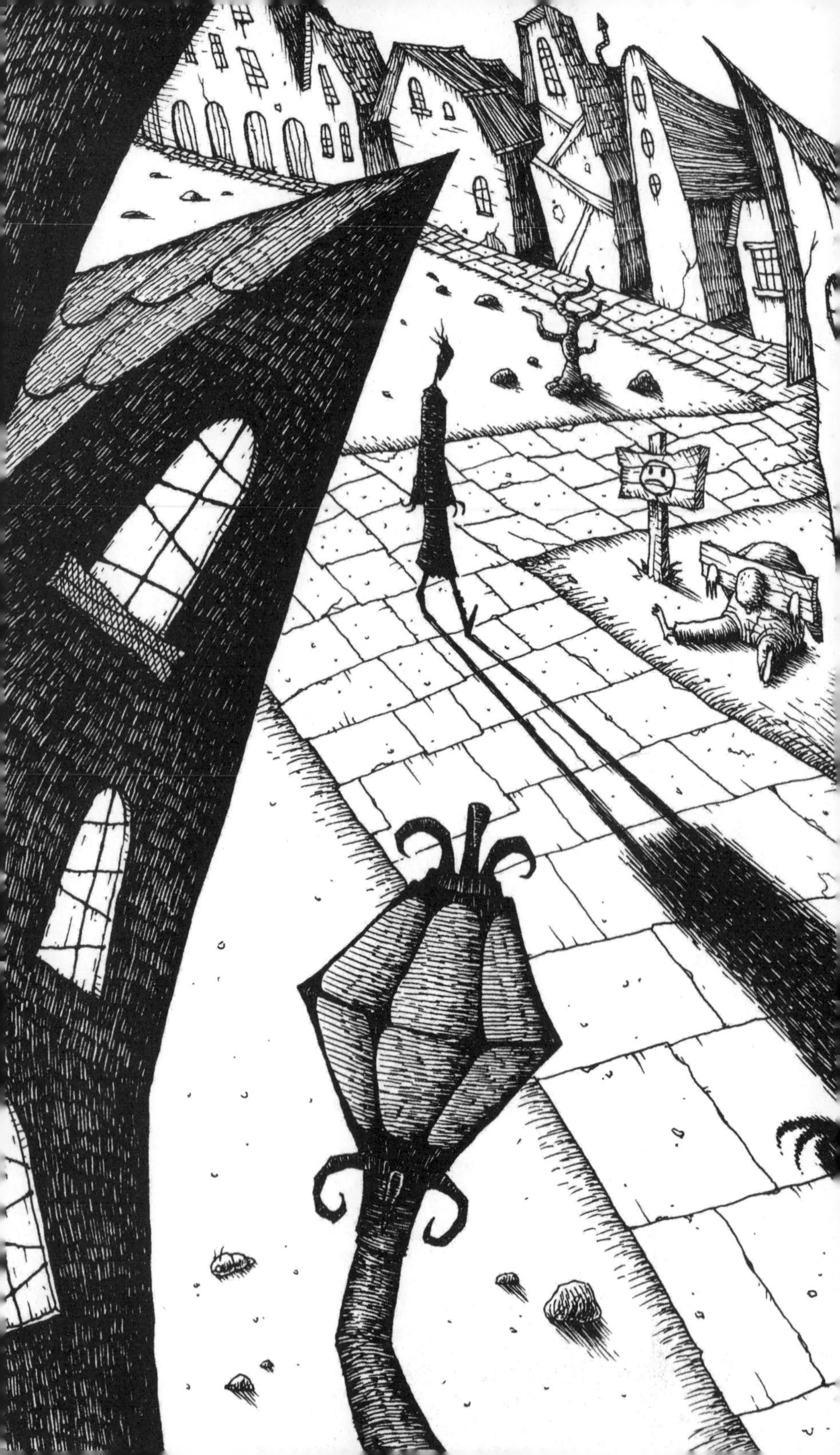

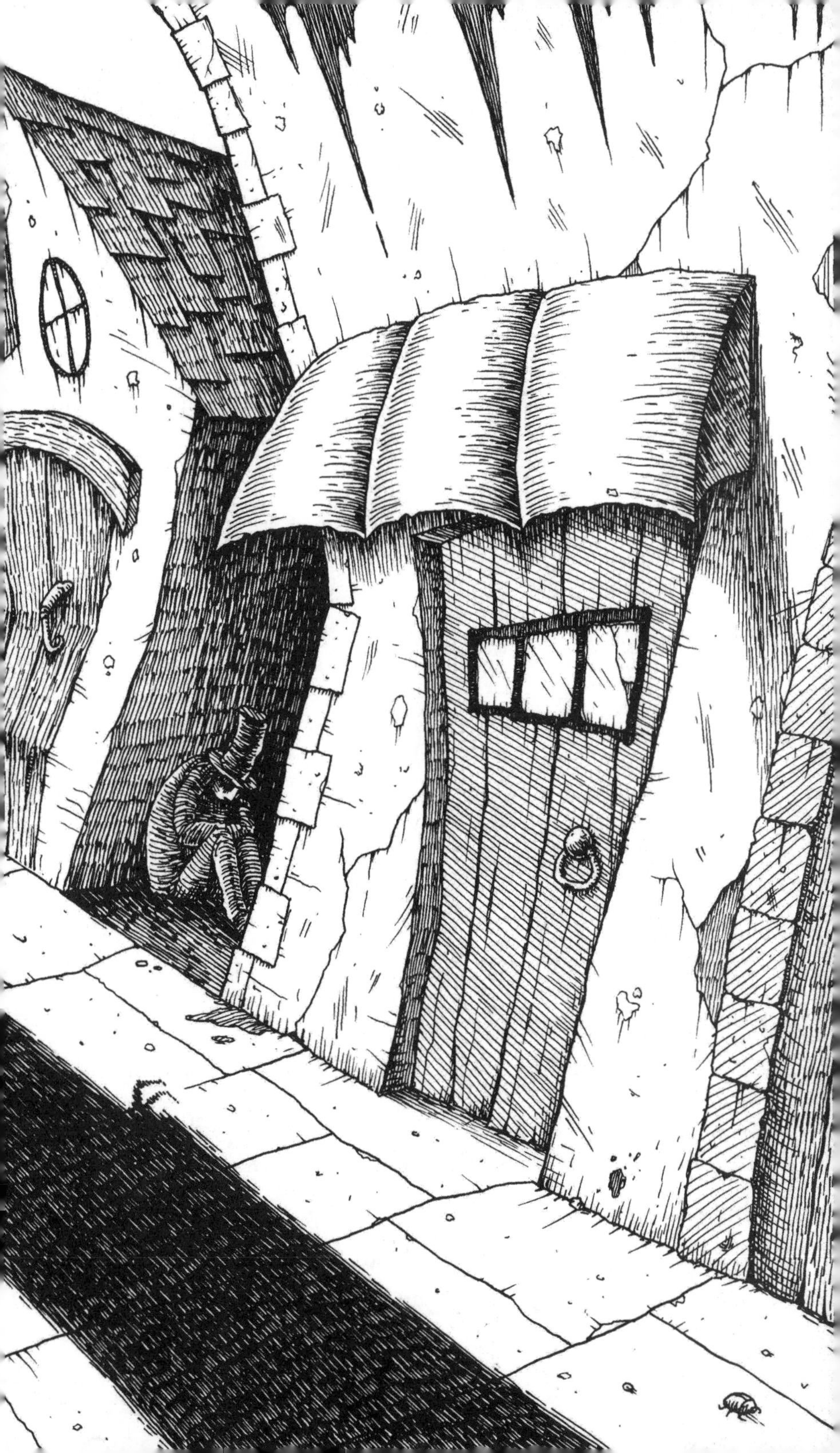

Zazil's ignorance of the whole story provided him with a certain amount of comfort, but sometimes he wondered why the good luck charms were such a necessity and why he was cursed with such hideous luck. However, since his mother's death he took his birthday ritual very seriously because he blamed himself. He knew he had to buy himself a charm before he went to work at the factory, even if it made him late.

He laced up his boots and fastened the clasps on his coat and made his way into the gray, misty gloom of the morning. Jagged, tall buildings loomed precariously through the mist overhead as he walked down the crooked, zigzagging road in search of a shop that would provide him with what he needed. Stopping at a large window with wrought iron bars protecting it from harm, he noticed the word "CURIO" on a decaying sign above it. "Perfect!" Zazil exclaimed as he opened the massive doors.

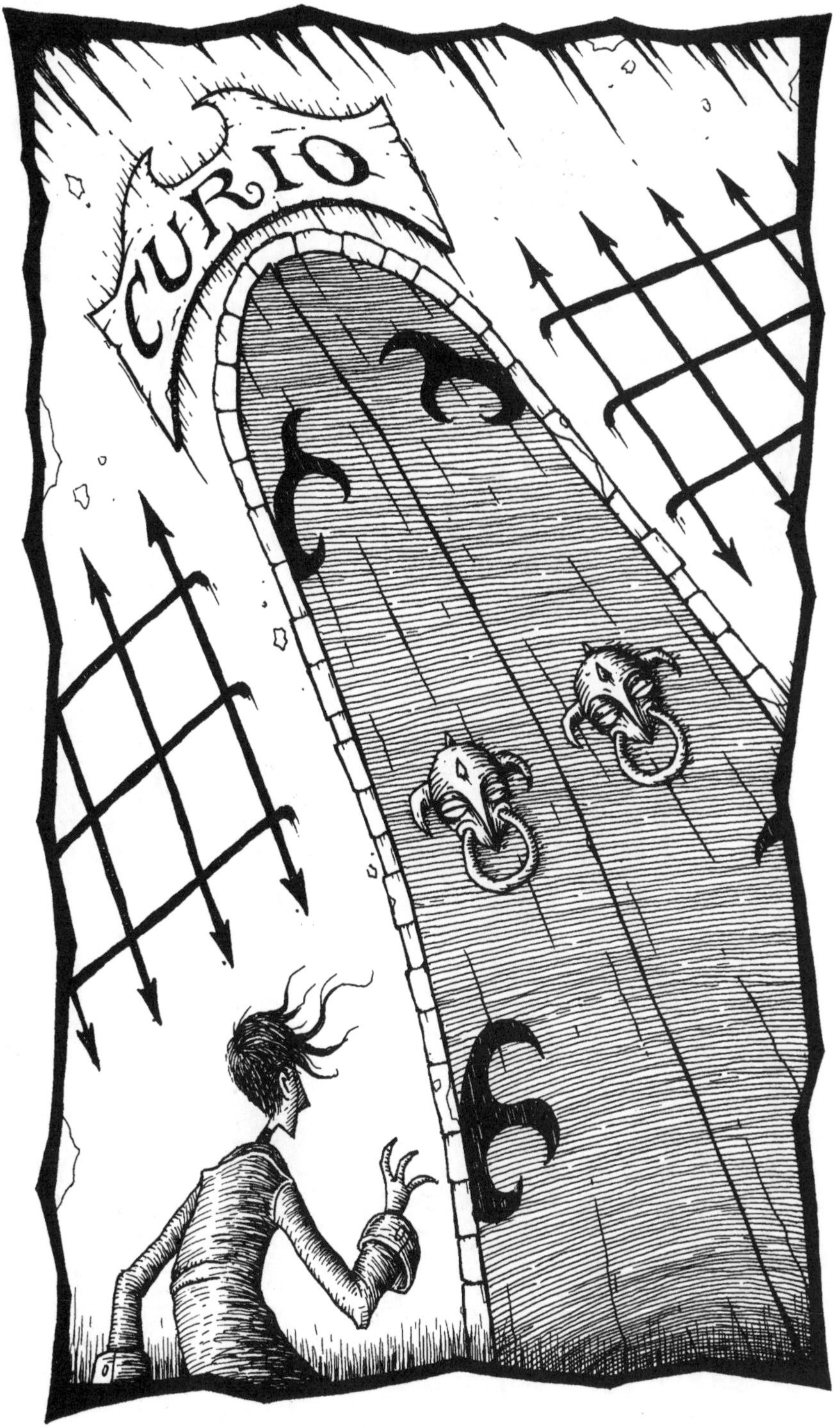
CURIO

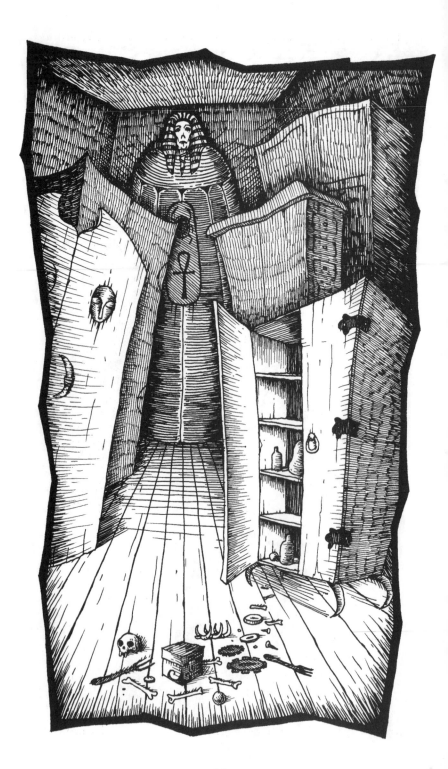

Upon entering the small, dusty shop, he was surrounded by objects both curious and strange. There were cabinets everywhere filled with oddities. He opened the closest one to him and was startled by a loud crash as several small objects hit the wooden floor. Looking down at the ground, he saw that the cabinet had contained an eclectic collection of random junk, including many kinds of bones, silver forks, sprockets, gears and a small metal box.

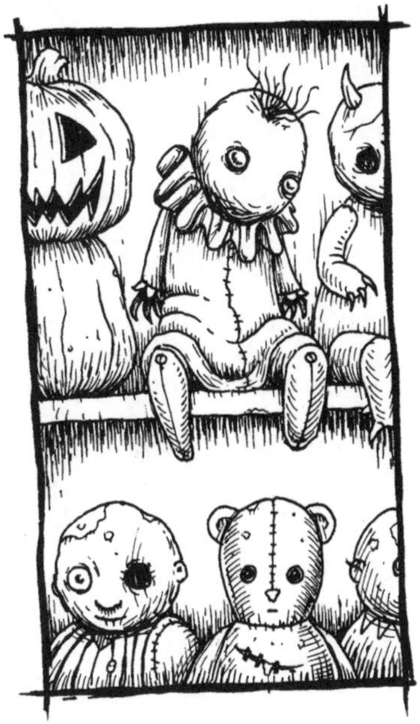

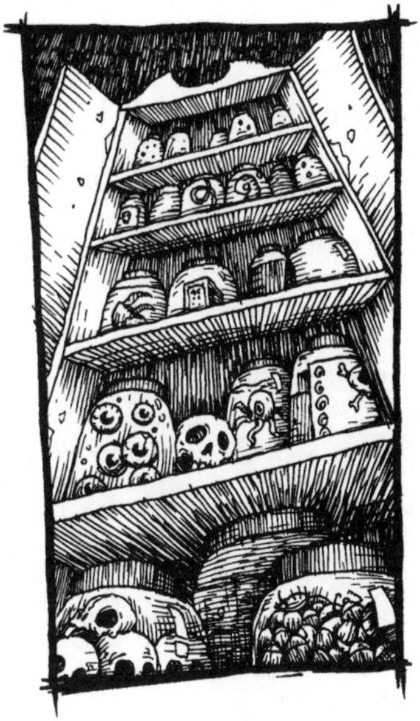

Nothing of use here, he thought. Moving on to the next cabinet he carefully opened the door only to discover it was full of old, crusty dolls. "Well maybe the next one," he sighed. Opening the huge doors of yet another cabinet, he found too many shelves filled with filthy jars containing everything from small skulls to human eyes floating in greenish liquid. Frustrated, Zazil finally started on his way out of the shop.

"Wait!" muttered an ancient-sounding voice. "I think I know what you seek." Suddenly, a withered old man appeared from behind a cabinet. "Look in the coffin back there," he said, pointing.

With nothing to lose but time, Zazil shuffled to the back of the shop to find a rotting sarcophagus made from a dark metal inlaid with silver. The intricate lid was already half-way open, so he reached inside. He found one solitary artifact on a shelf inside, and pulled it out to examine it. The trinket was a small scarab beetle with wings carved from hematite and inlaid with silver and obsidian, very much like the sarcophagus that hid it. "This is it!" yelled Zazil.

"You can have it if you like it that much. I can't seem to get rid of the thing. It almost seems as though people are scared of it," said the shopkeeper in a weary voice.

"Thank you!" replied Zazil. Looking at the clock, he realized that he was over an hour late to work. He despised his job, so it was easy to lose track of time. "Excuse me, I really have to get going!" he shouted.

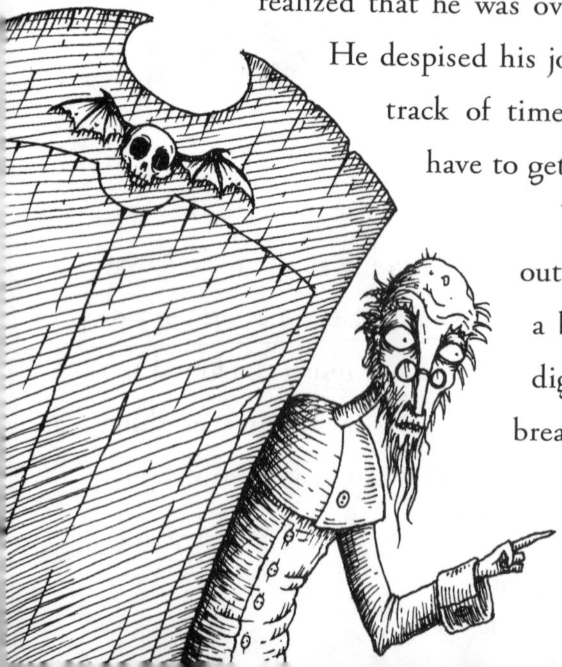

With his second step outside, he was greeted with a bomb in the form of the digested remains of a bird's breakfast. And so started another typical day in the town.

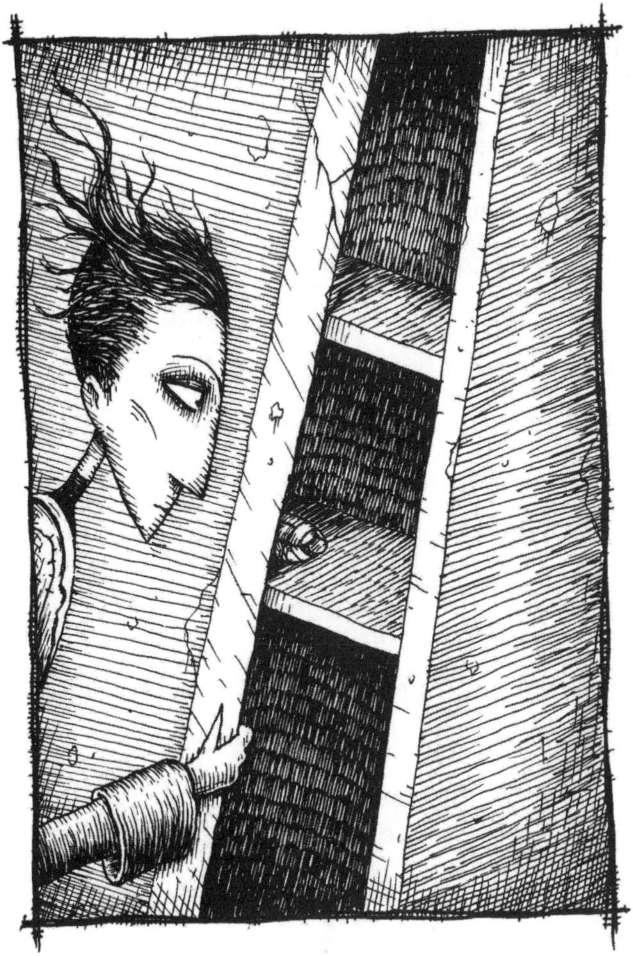

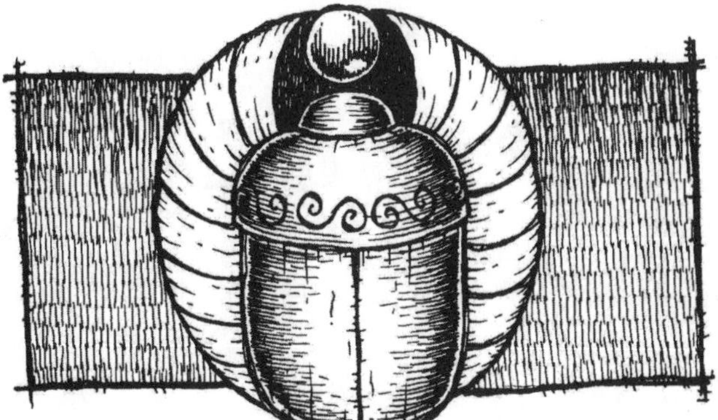

Rushing as fast as he could, Zazil made his way to the factory where he worked. It was a gigantic structure with towering smoke stacks that spewed forth a dark, ominous cloud the color of death. Zazil sneaked around to one of the side doors and quietly slipped in. Once inside, he followed the stairs down to the lower level where he worked. The air was thick with smoke and the sounds of the gears that never stopped turning. Carefully, he sneaked past his fellow workers and settled into his work station. He put on his gloves and goggles and began his mind-numbingly boring task of checking each part for defects. He hated his job with a passion, but he had no other alternative. He had begun working there at the age of 13, after his mother died. Having no other skills to speak of, he felt that he was stuck there.

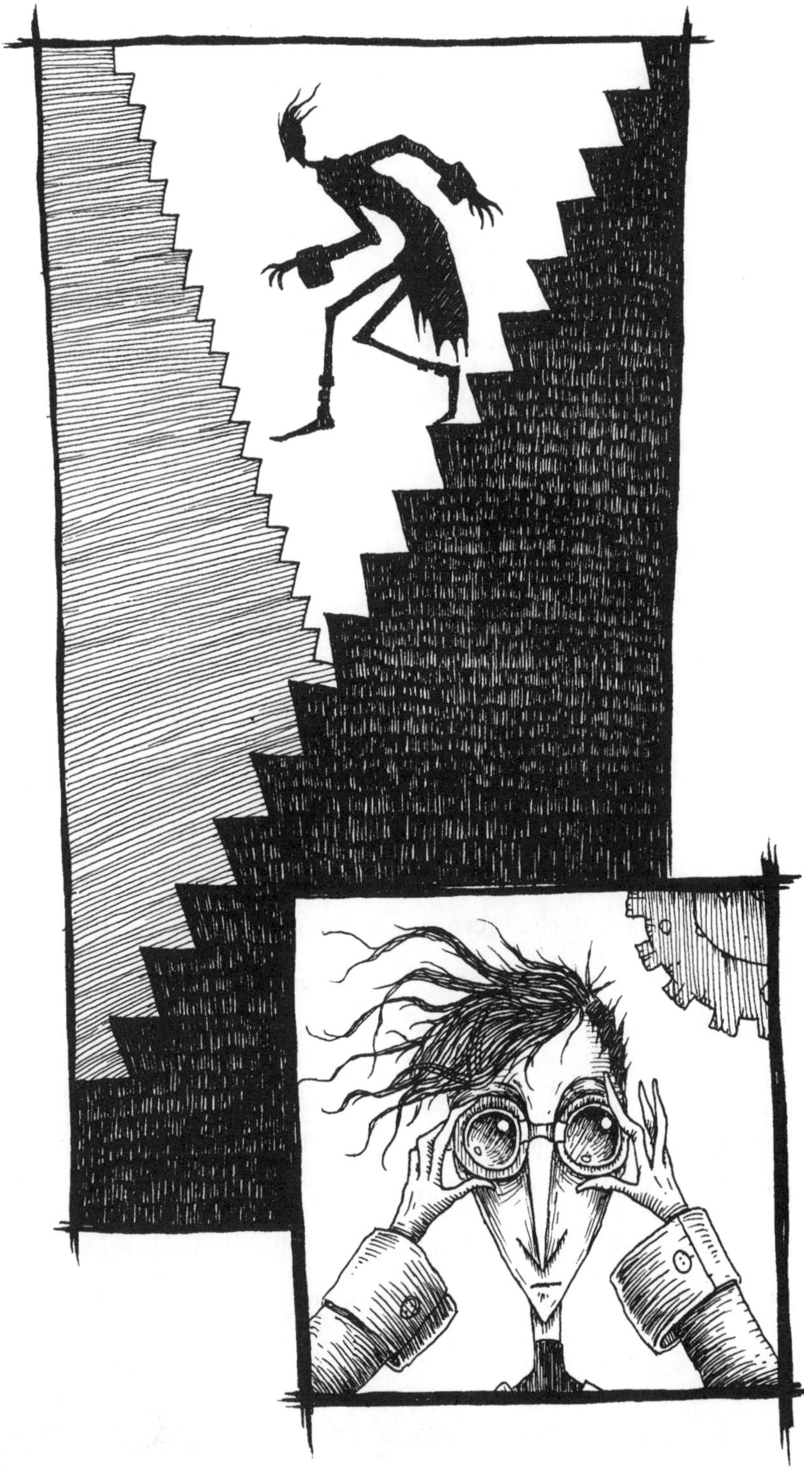

Just as he thought he had entered unnoticed, he heard a loud, raspy voice shout, "Zazil! Where the hell have you been?!" It was his assholic boss, Mr. Teaskin.

"I apologize, sir. I was not feeling well this morning," replied Zazil.

"Well, is that so? With you being as slow as you are, every second counts. Besides, you'd be surprised at how much better you'll feel after a little work," responded Teaskin in a patronizing tone.

"I will stay later today if it will help," said Zazil.

"No, I have a better idea. How about I dock two weeks worth of pay? One week to make up for your tardiness and another for your lack of speed," his boss said.

At that moment something inside Zazil broke, and with a red face full of rage, he screamed in an acidic tone, "GO TO HELL, TEASKIN! I QUIT!" Pushing his surprised boss aside, he stormed out of the building.

Upon leaving the factory, Zazil realized that his decision may have been a rash one. How would he make a living? Would he lose his flat and become homeless? He didn't really know. The thought of all of this brought a melancholy mood over him that he couldn't shake. On top of all of this, it was his birthday, which also meant that it was the anniversary of his mother's death. Another part of his birthday ritual was to visit her grave, so he began his journey to the cemetery.

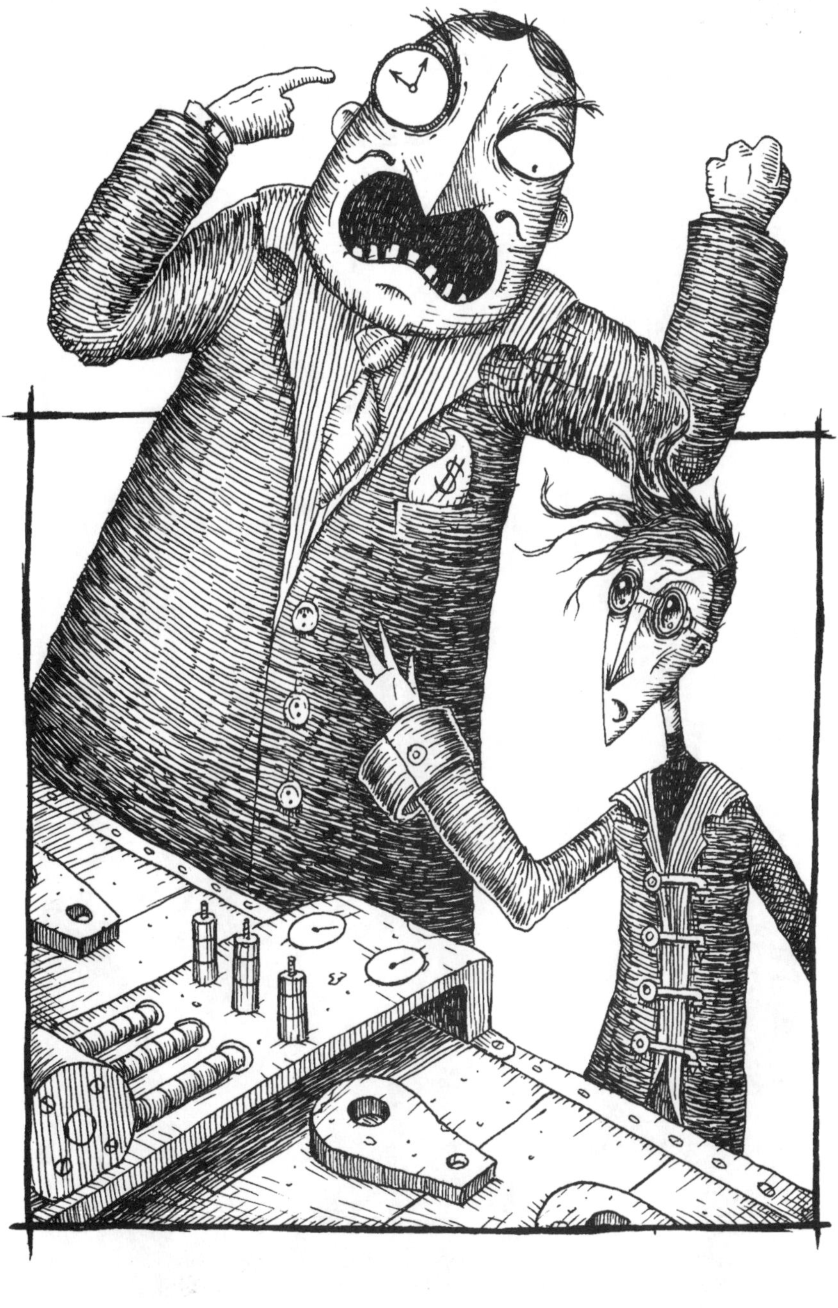

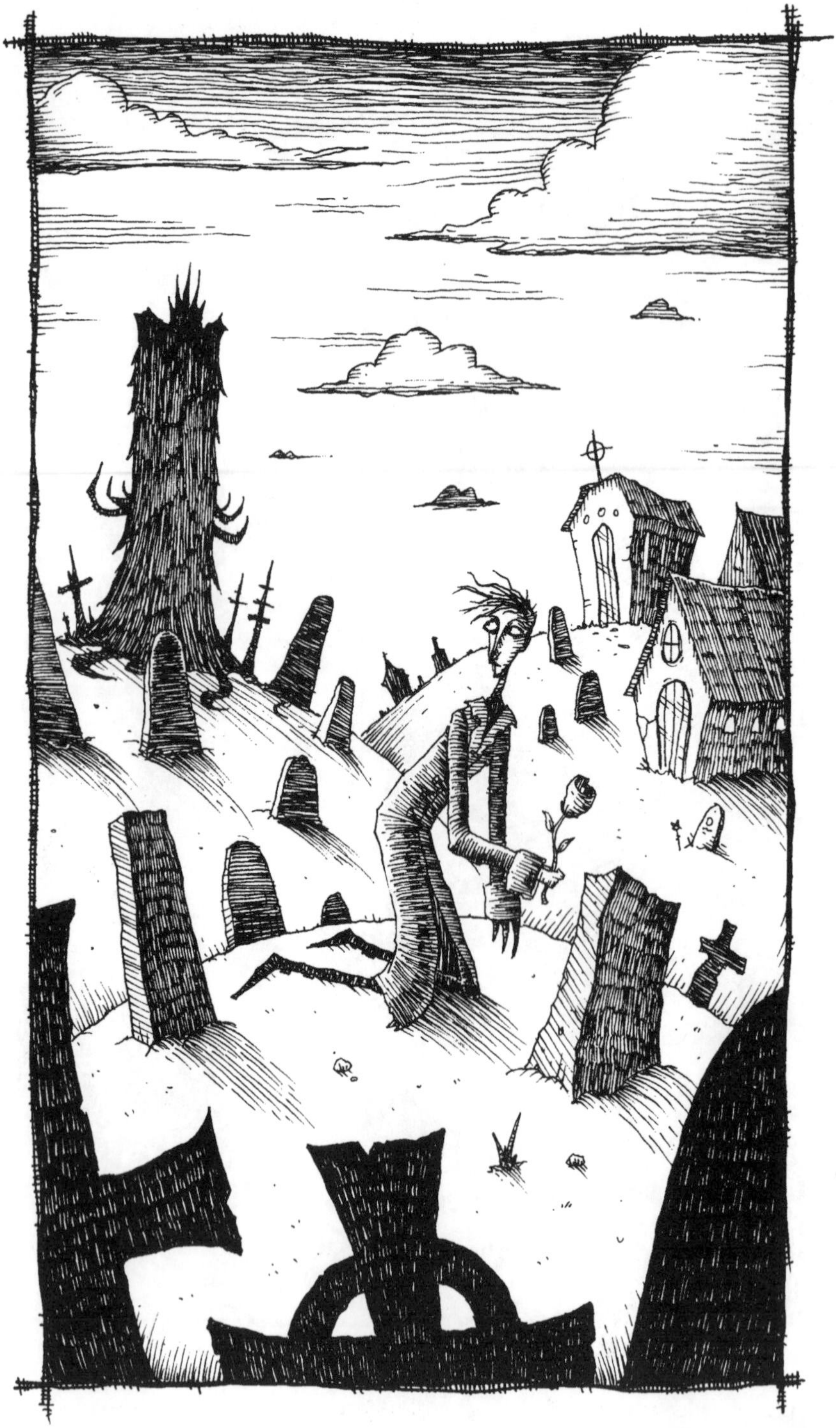

The air in the cemetery was clean, crisp and cold, and the quality of light that washed over the graves and tombstones had a monochromatic beauty. Zazil felt calm and at peace here. He found his mother's grave and placed a flower on it. As he sat down beside her grave marker, he noticed a shadow moving quickly through the cemetery. He got up abruptly and looked all around him. Nothing appeared to be there. Then, suddenly, he heard the rustle of dry leaves. He turned around quickly to see what lurked behind him. Whatever it was, it was big. All Zazil could make out of the creature, which was wrapped entirely in dark, tattered robes, were the sharp, talon-like claws that protruded from its sleeves.

The creature realized its cover had been blown, so it lunged forward to attack. Zazil quickly jumped out of the way and climbed up on top of one of the larger mausoleums to safety. The creature followed his every move, and within seconds it was up there with him. At that moment, looking to the sky, Zazil thought that it might be the end. Then he heard a cracking noise. It was the roof caving in! He leapt to the ground as the whole mausoleum came crashing down, and

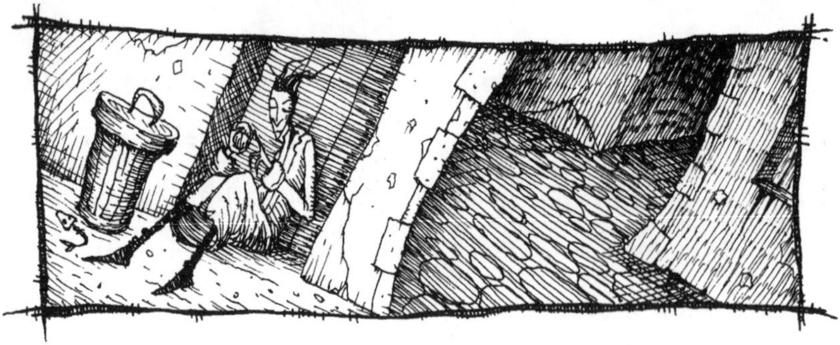

the creature with it. This caused a chain reaction with the mausoleum next to it, knocking it down as well. The monster was dead! dead! dead!

Lying on the ground next to the creature's corpse was a small trinket similar to the good luck charm he had found before work that morning. He decided to take it as kind of a trophy for slaying the beast. After grabbing the amulet he decided it not wise to hang around, so he left.

Where should I go now? Zazil thought. Part of him still had the fear that there may have been more of these things after him, so he hurried into the hidden alleyways that he knew well.

It was getting dark enough to hide, so he sat in an alcove and examined

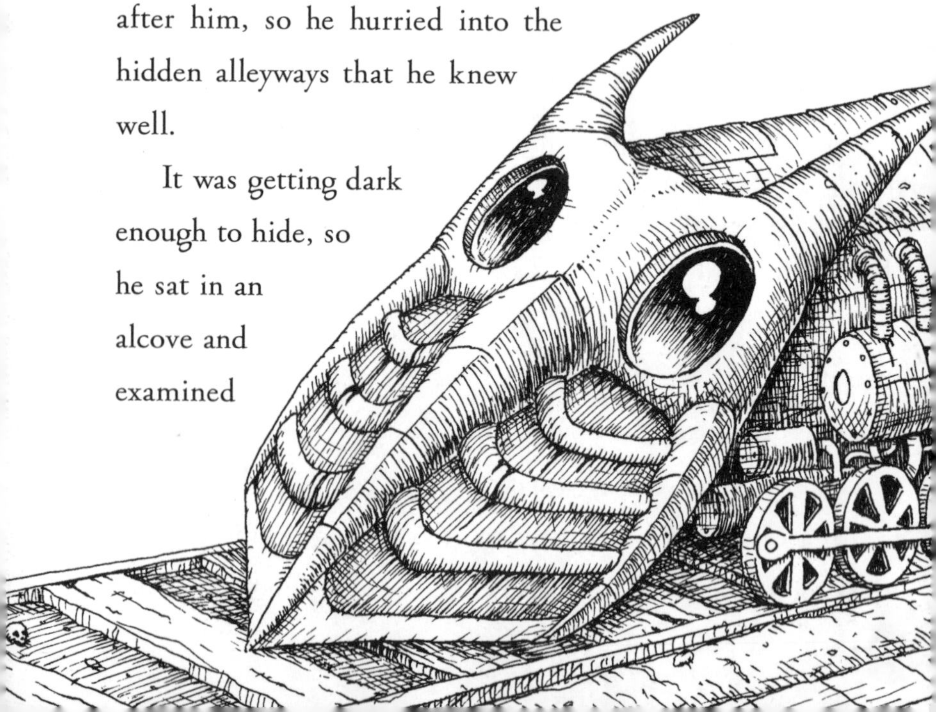

the stolen artifact. It looked as if the same person who had made his scarab had made this amulet also. It too looked like it was made from a dark metallic stone, then inlaid with silver and obsidian.

Just as he was returning the charms to his coat pocket, Zazil heard the familiar train noise, far in the distance. Turning around, he saw something he had never noticed before, an ornate train station.

"Hmmm, must have just opened," he said to himself. Interested, he walked over and sat on a bench. He saw lights approaching as the train noise grew louder, and the massive steam locomotive came grinding to a halt at the station.

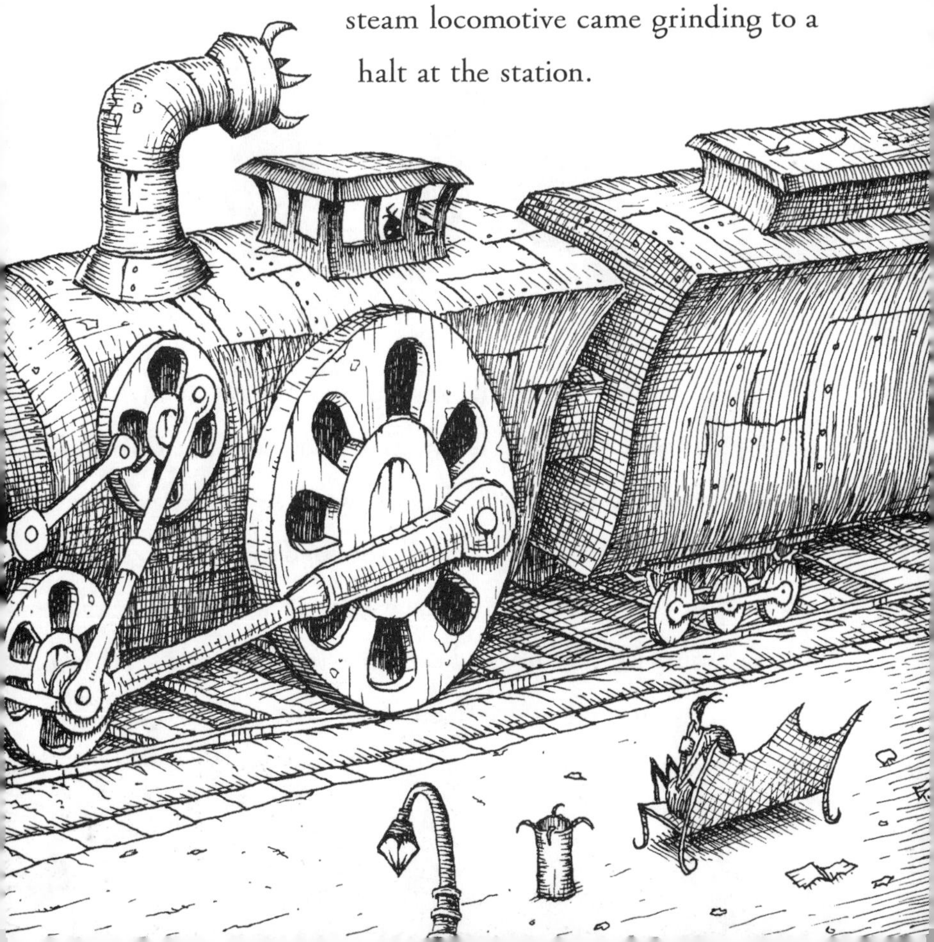

The train had stopped, yet no one got on or off. With perhaps another rash decision, Zazil boarded the train, not caring where it took him. Inside were several passengers of many sizes. One man's head touched the ceiling. With closer observation, Zazil realized that it was not a man at all, but some kind of horned creature in man-style clothing. He was frightened at first, but it was too late. The train was moving.

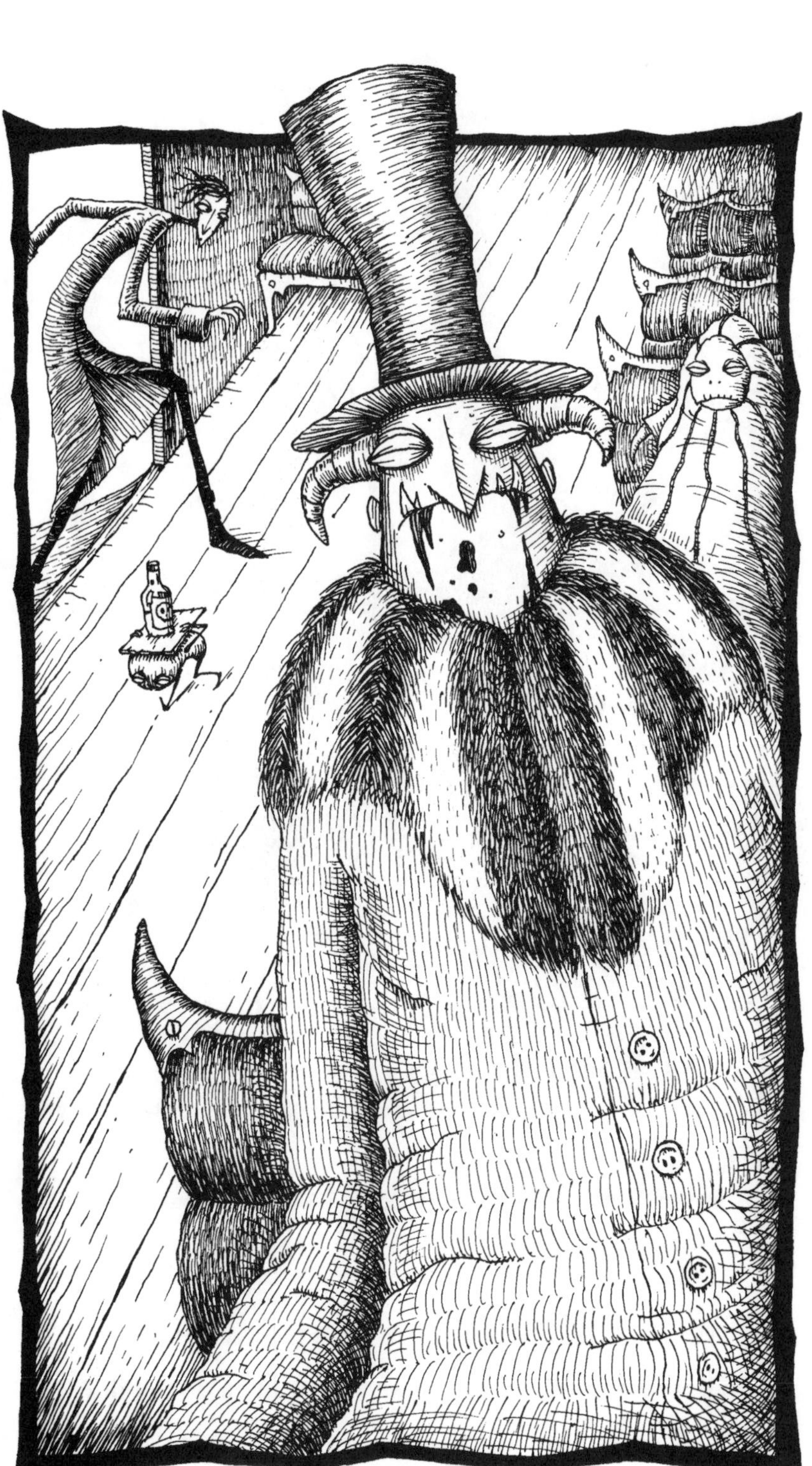

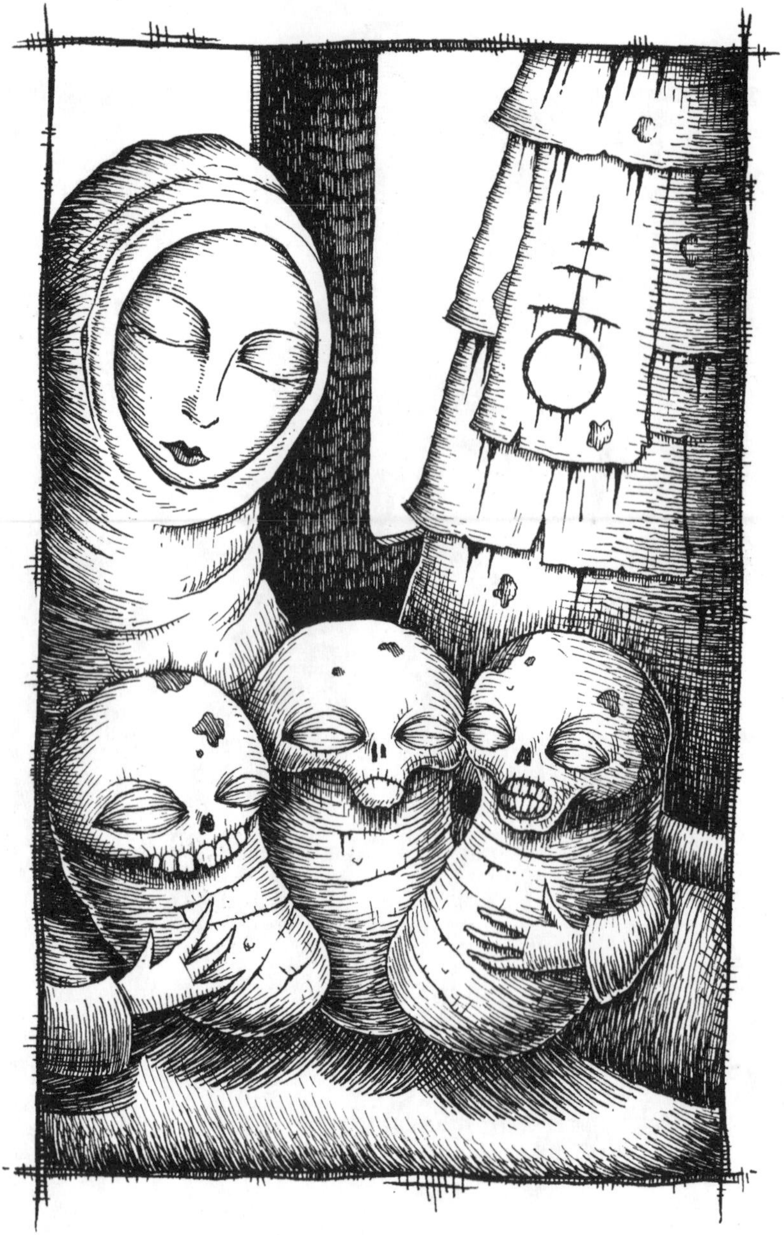

No one on the train seemed to notice Zazil. It was as if he weren't even there. It was with this that he realized that he was not in peril. He decided to just sit back and enjoy the ride. As he looked around him a mother with three very small infants caught his eye. A closer look revealed that the children were

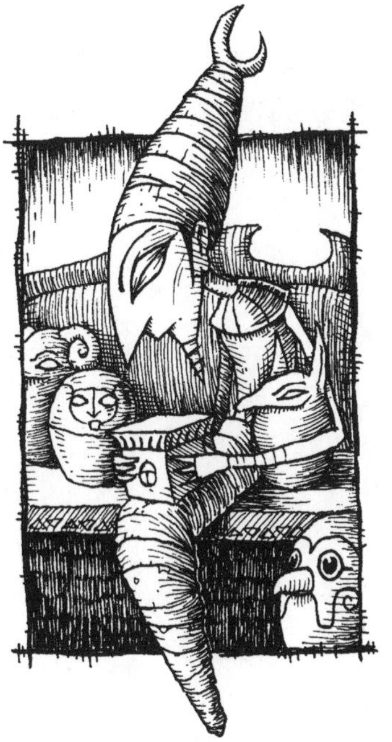

mummified and dusty, with dry, shriveled faces, yet somehow still alive. Sitting behind her was a monstrous thing covered in oily black armor. Behind him sat a man with four jars carved from exotic stones. He held in his lap an elaborately carved wooden box. From time to time he would open it to reveal several tiny men carved from stone. The men in the box squirmed around and tried to escape when the box was opened. Zazil wondered how he was making the little stone men animate as he surrendered to sleep....

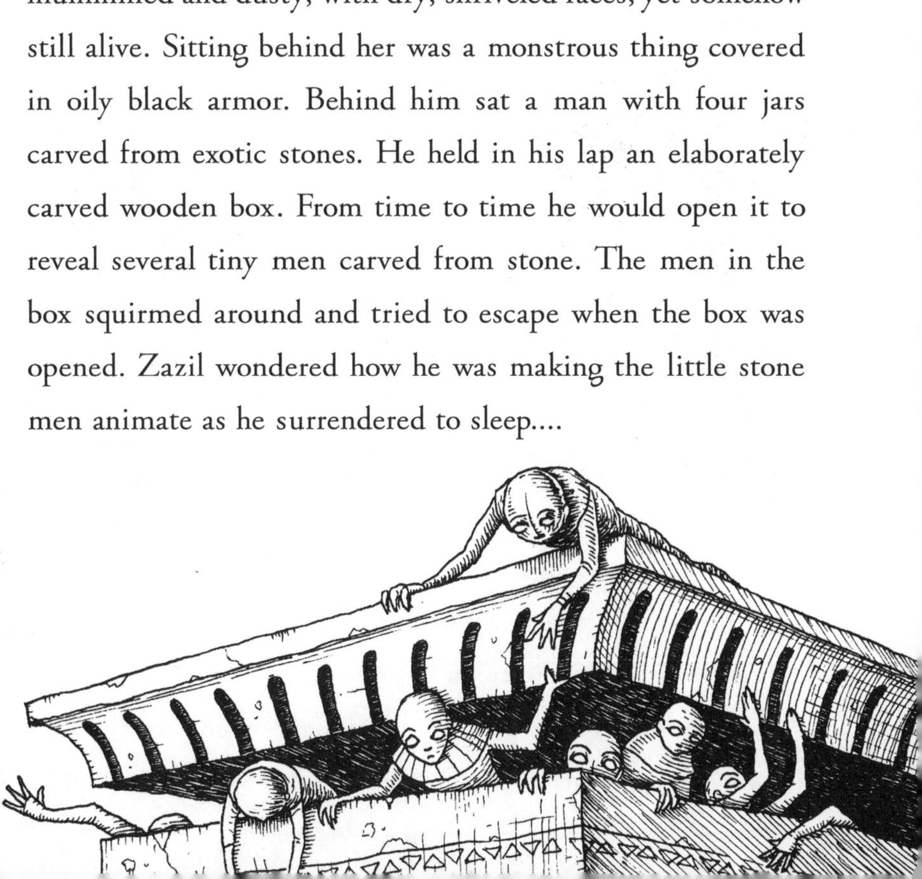

Zazil awoke to the screeching sound of the train arriving at the next stop. He found himself alone in the car. Everyone else seemed to have vanished, but, looking out the window, he saw nothing. The door slid open and another passenger boarded. Zazil, being a bit introverted, tried his best to ignore him and not to make eye contact.

As the new passenger took his seat, right in front of him, Zazil noticed an object in his hand very much like the two scarabs he possessed. Curious, he mustered up the courage

to speak to the man. He tapped the hooded stranger on the shoulder, who then turned to face him. Zazil was startled at his appearance. The man's face seemed artificial, as if it were carved from wood. "I noticed the artifact in your hand. Do you mind if I ask how you got it?" inquired Zazil.

"If I told you, you wouldn't believe me," the strange man answered.

"I've been riding a train full of monsters and mummy children. At this point I think I'd believe anything," responded Zazil.

"Well, it all started when I was captured by these monstrous things that caged me up for transport to their factory. What they didn't know was that I had a very weak heart. The stress of all this was a bit much for me to take, and I died during transport. They disposed of my corpse, but my ghost remained. I listened closely to their conversations and learned that they were creatures from Hell secretly created by

demons to do their grunt work in a soul-processing factory."

"What do they want with us?" asked Zazil.

"I'm not quite sure. I stuck around just long enough to steal this beetle-looking thing," responded the ghost man as he held up the amulet that was almost identical to Zazil's. As he did so, the face-like mask slid down, revealing an almost transparent head with skeletal features and hollows where eyes should have been. Having never seen a ghost, Zazil stared, petrified, as the spirit pulled down his hood to adjust his human-faced mask.

As Zazil spoke to the apparition, hunger pains began to stab at him. He wasn't sure how long it had been since he'd eaten, but he felt as if he were going to pass out. He asked the ghost where he could find a bit to eat, but the ghost replied, "I'm dead. I don't get hungry anymore. In fact, I kind of miss the tastes and smells of food. If I were you I'd try getting off at the next stop. I've seen small towns and villages with markets and restaurants along the way."

Zazil took his advice. At the next stop, he bid his farewell to the dead man and got off the train.

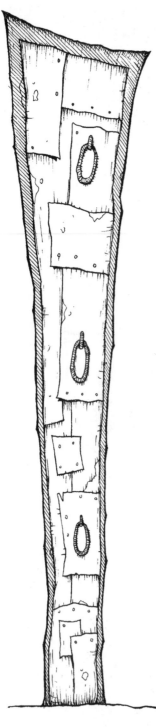

Having exited the train car, Zazil entered a large, empty room full of exceedingly tall doors. Figuring that what he needed was on the other side, he grabbed one of the huge, rusted metal handles and proceeded to venture outside. As soon as he closed the door, he realized it may have been a big mistake. In front of him lay a landscape of filth and misery. When he turned around, the door, the walls and the entire station disappeared. He was trapped.

Still hungry, he started to explore. The first thing he noticed was the horrible stench of rotting flesh. There were carcasses everywhere, and the only vegetation he observed were severely twisted trees and slimy, smelly plants that looked as if they were made of meat. He kept walking, figuring that he would eventually find his way out.

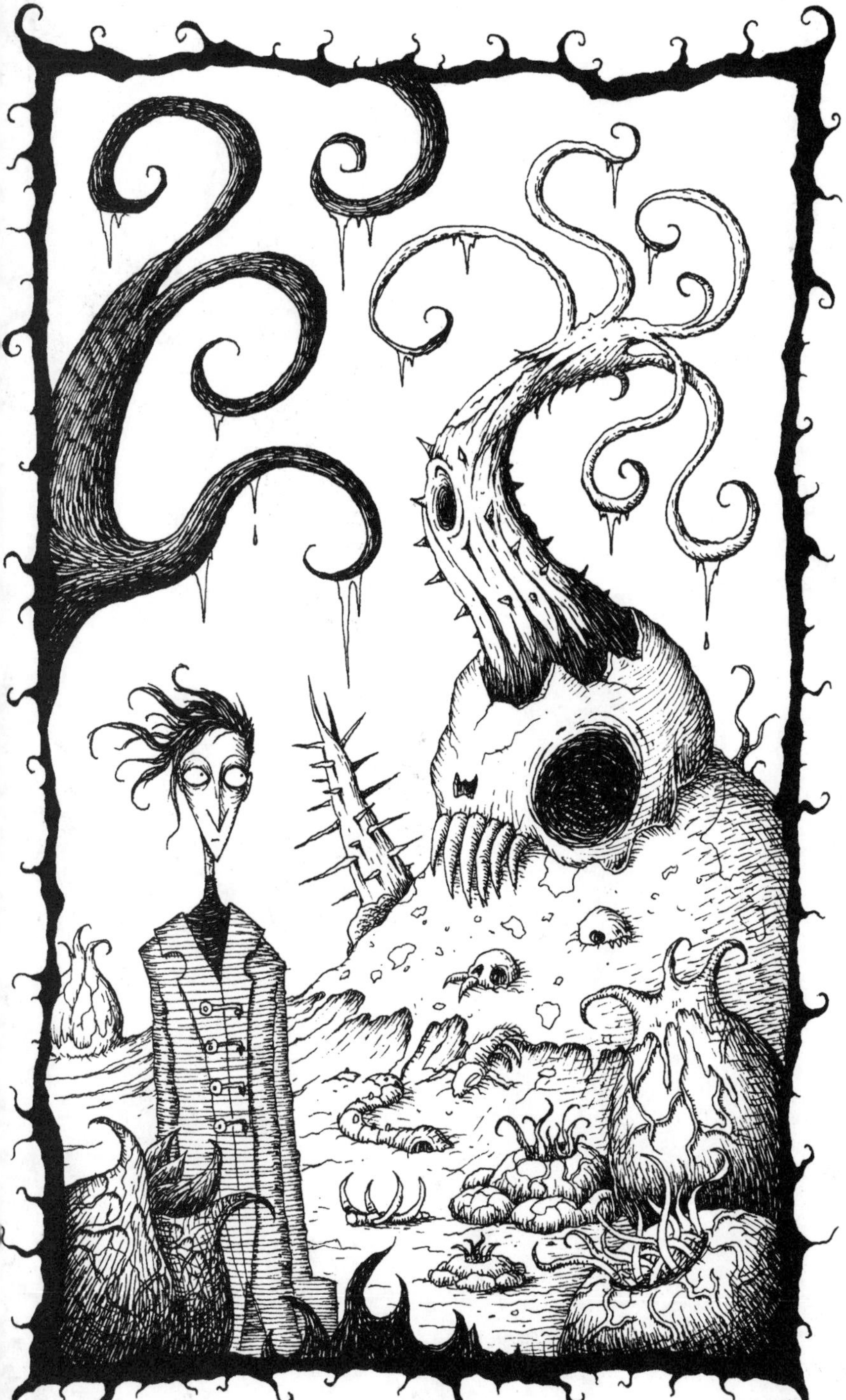

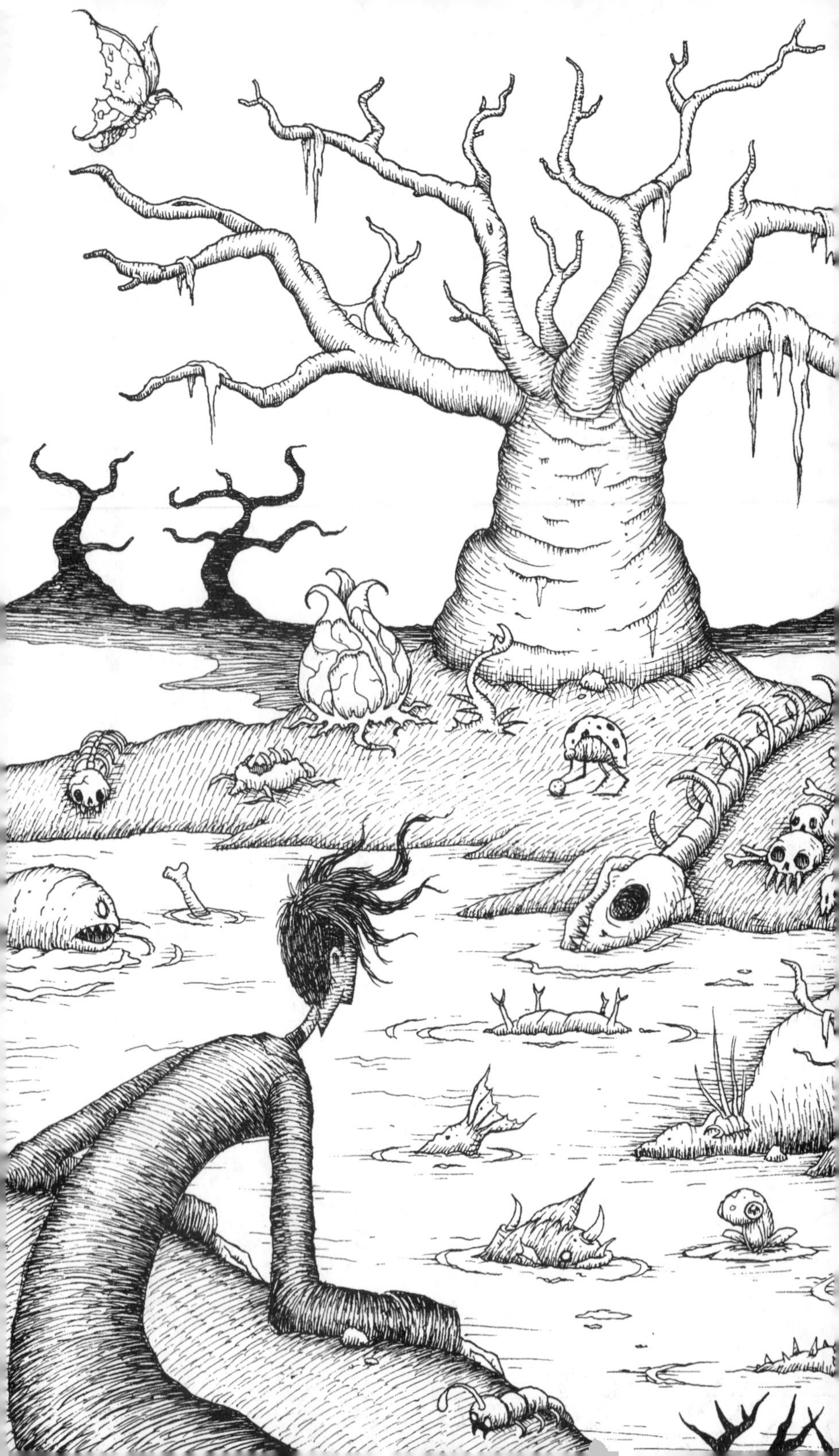

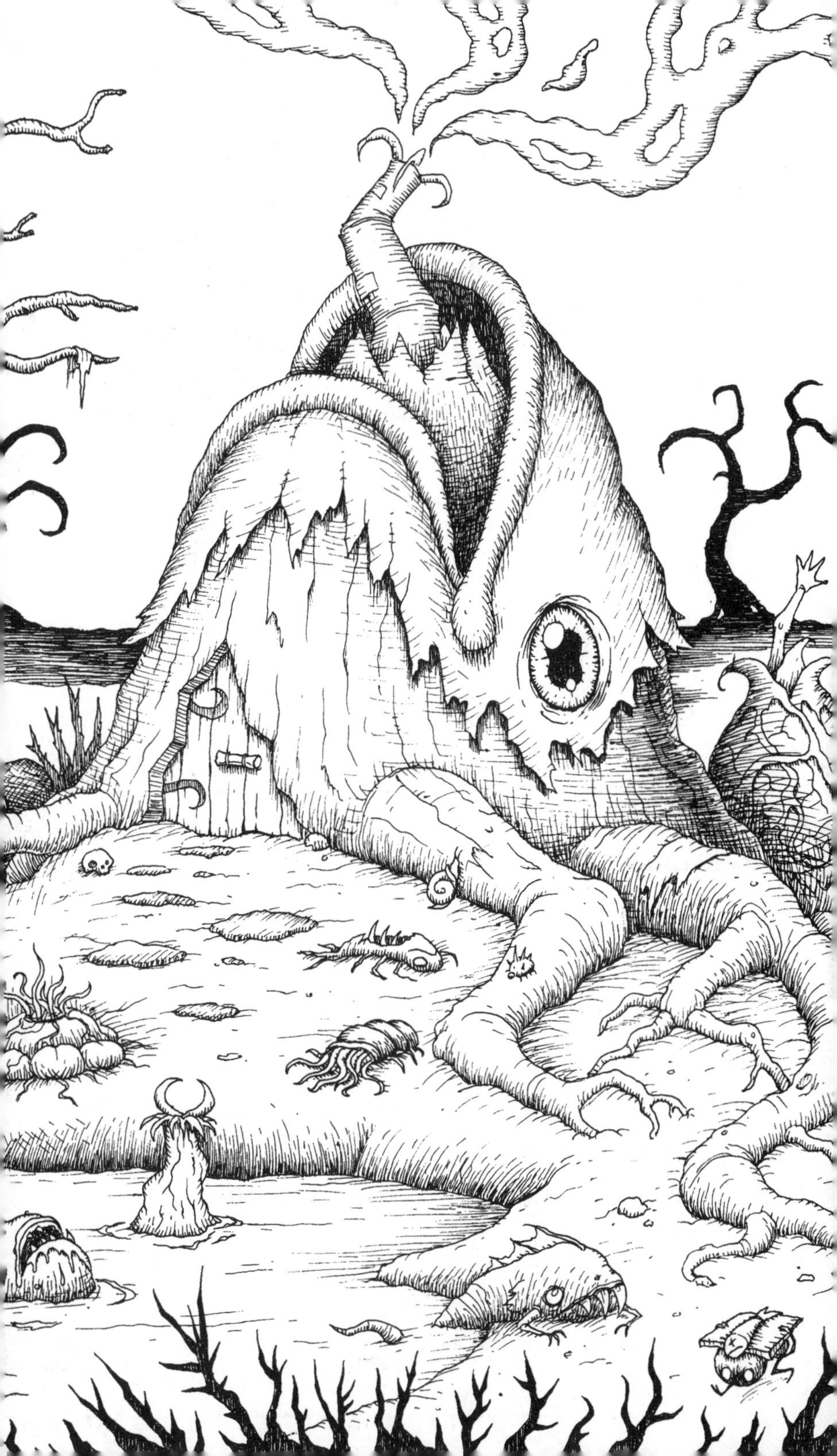

After seemingly endless walking, Zazil approached what appeared to be a hut of some kind. As he got closer, he saw that it was composed of a huge fish head stretched over a hollowed-out tree stump. There was smoke ascending from the mouth of the fish, so he figured that someone was inside. He knocked on the door several times, but no one answered. From inside he could hear the faint sound of someone weeping. This time he shouted, "HELLO, ANYONE THERE?"

Still, no one answered. Then, just as he turned around the front door slowly creaked open. Standing in the doorway was one of the most pathetic creatures he had ever seen. Its face was corroded with tears.

"Wh, wh, whooz there?" wheezed the sad little thing.

"I'm Zazil."

"You're here to kill me, aren't you?" it sighed.

"No, actually, I was hoping you could help me find my way out of this place," said Zazil.

At that moment the little thing burst into tears.

"What's wrong?" asked Zazil.

"I've been exiled here," the little creature choked out between tears.

"I'm sorry to hear that," said Zazil. "You must have

committed a pretty heinous crime to have been sent out here."

"I guess so... if you consider being afraid to die a crime," sobbed the creature.

"I don't understand," replied Zazil.

"Well, at a certain age we Nogs are taught to travel to other dimensions. If we don't go we're considered disgraceful and our elders give us the choice to die or be exiled. I didn't want to die, so I was sent here," finished the Nog.

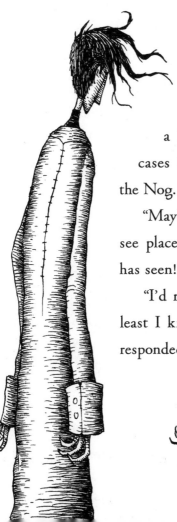

"What's so bad about traveling to other dimensions?" asked Zazil.

"We can't always control whether or not we end up in a hostile environment. In some cases it's instant suicide," answered the Nog.

"Maybe it's worth it... You'd get to see places and things that no one else has seen!" said Zazil.

"I'd rather stay here, thank you. At least I know what to expect," the Nog responded.

Looking around at the decaying carcasses and carnivorous plants, Zazil decided that he'd rather take his chances with death than stay in this place.

"Well, in any case, I need to get out of here," said Zazil.

"Why the rush?" asked the Nog. "You just got here. Besides, you're the only visitor I've had. Why don't you come inside for a bite to eat? Surely you're hungry after your long journey."

Zazil *was* very hungry, so even though the horrible, smelly environment bothered him, he decided to stay for a bit. The inside of the Nog's hut was primitive, but surprisingly clean and organized. There was a small bed on one side, fashioned out of bones and wood and covered with the pelt of an animal of unknown origin. Toward the center of the room was a crude, wooden table with two chairs, as if the Nog had been expecting company. On top of it rested a lantern and a few spoons made of dark wood. Built into the back wall out of stone was a fireplace that housed a rusted cauldron hanging over an open flame.

"Have a seat," said the Nog as he picked up two wooden bowls.

"Don't mind if I do," replied Zazil just as the Nog placed two steaming bowls of thick brown goo in front of him. The soup that the Nog had prepared smelled pungent, but tasted quite good. Zazil thought that perhaps his hunger had affected his sense of taste.

During their meal Zazil spoke of the creatures from Hell

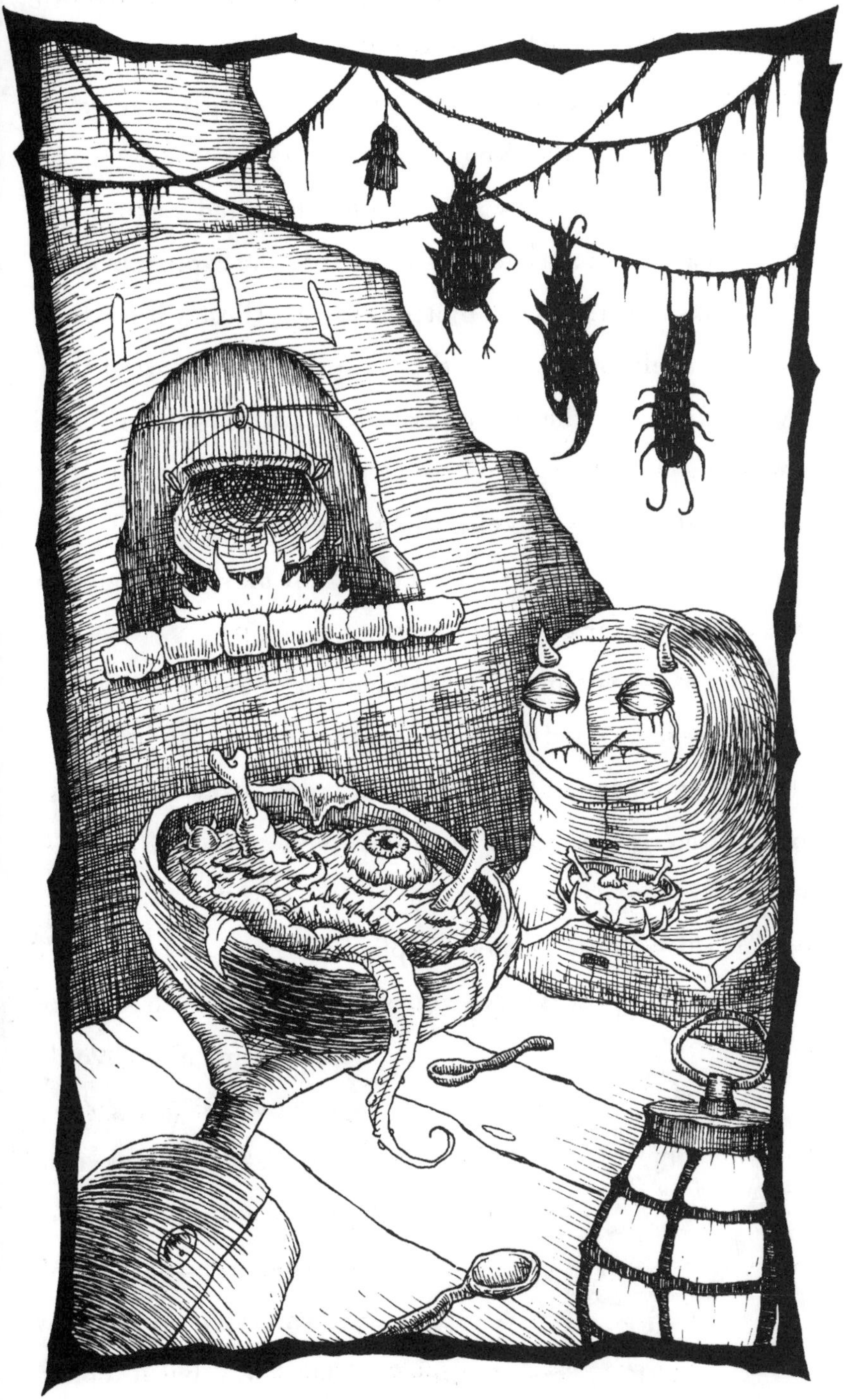

that pursued him. The Nog's face turned even more pale when Zazil asked if he knew of them.

"I've heard stories about vengeful beings known as 'Charnoks'," said the Nog.

"What do you know about them?" inquired Zazil.

"I heard from another Nog who had been captured by the Charnoks that they were plotting against those who created them in Hell. Supposedly, the Charnoks have started their own factory, and they enslave other creatures for labor," said the Nog.

"What do they make in this factory?"

"Maybe weapons to get back at their makers. Whatever the case, I prefer to stay away from them."

"Are they part of the reason you stay here?"

"They're as good a reason as any!"

"You mentioned that you were taught how to travel to other dimensions. Does that mean you could leave here?" asked Zazil.

"Yes, I suppose I could," replied the Nog.

"Then suppose I gave you something in exchange for

teaching me how. Would you show me?" asked Zazil as he held the trinket he had stolen from the slain monster in his hand.

The Nog didn't know what it was, but it looked

40

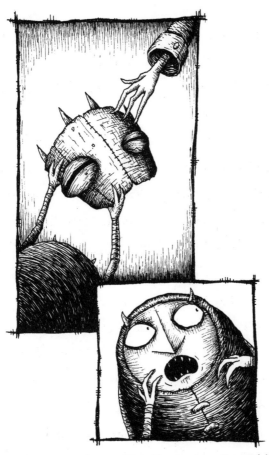

valuable, so he wanted it. "Yes, I suppose I could show you how," he said. "Right... Let's get started!" He ran to the back of his horrible fish hut and quickly reemerged with a mask.

"What's that for?" asked Zazil.

"We can't perform the ritual with out the essential tools, and this is one of them. You'll also need a stick. Any one will do," replied the Nog. "First, put on the mask. Then, with the stick draw a rectangle just large enough for yourself. This will prevent anything larger than you from following. Next, walk around the rectangle three times. This should activate the portal." The Nog handed the mask to Zazil.

No sooner had Zazil received the mask than he noticed dark shapes looming behind him. He tried to run, but it was too late. The cowardly Nog screamed, "Charnoks!" and ran into the woods.

They were more creatures similar to the one he encountered in the cemetery. The bigger one grabbed him, while the smaller one took an amulet out of his pocket. As he did so, another train station appeared from the mist in the woods. After they boarded the train, the Charnoks crammed Zazil into a cage for transport.

Well, this is the end.... he thought as the train slowly chugged away from the station.

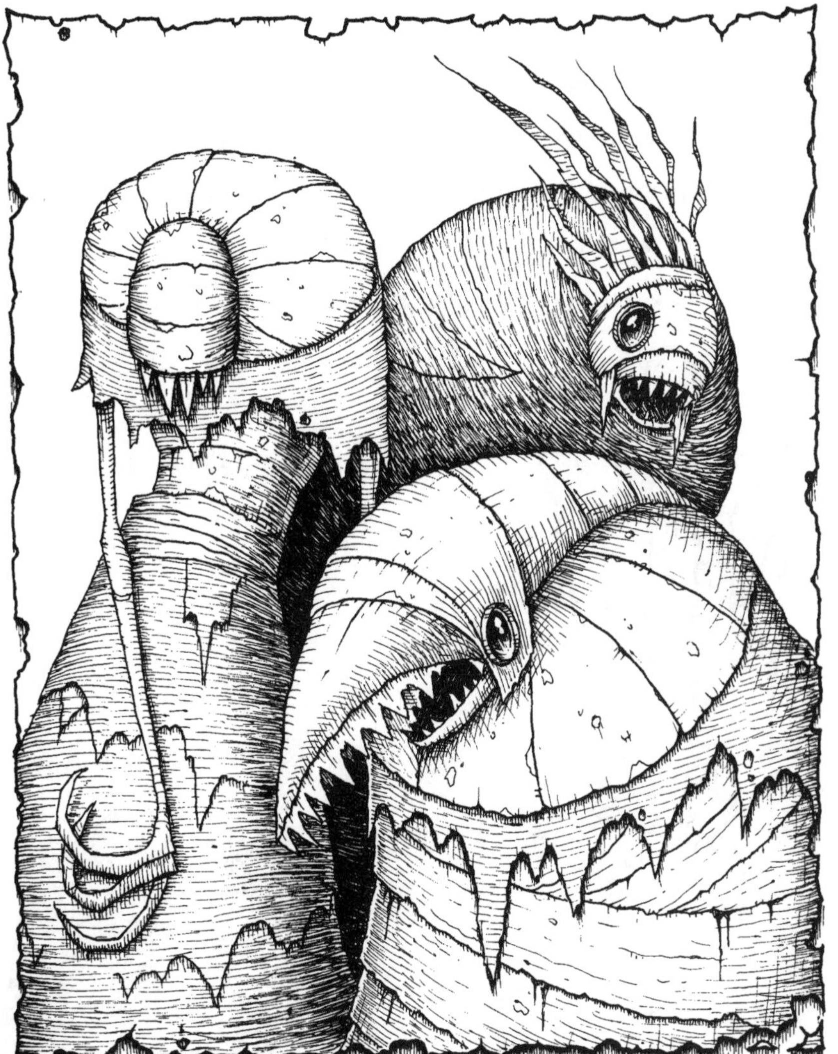

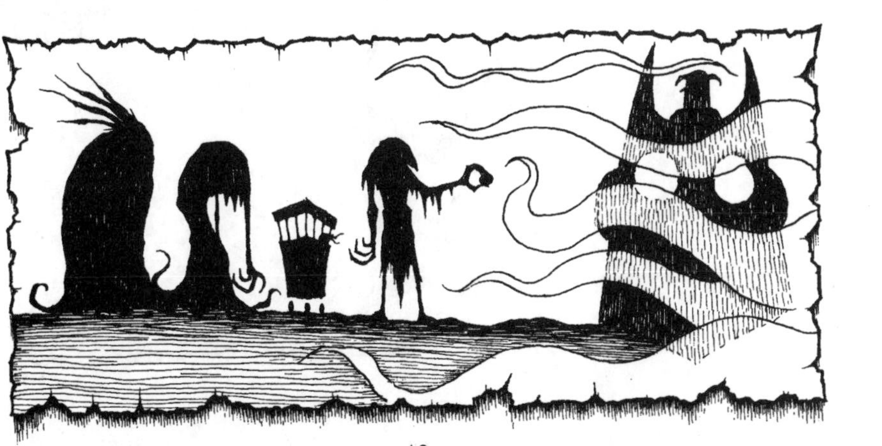

Once the train stopped, one of the Charnoks wheeled Zazil's cage down onto the platform. This station was different, though. It had no benches or doors that he could see. There were just holes in a metal floor.

Before Zazil had time to get his bearings, his cage was dropped down one of the holes, and he slid at breakneck speed down the metal tube as his metal cage emitted sparks.

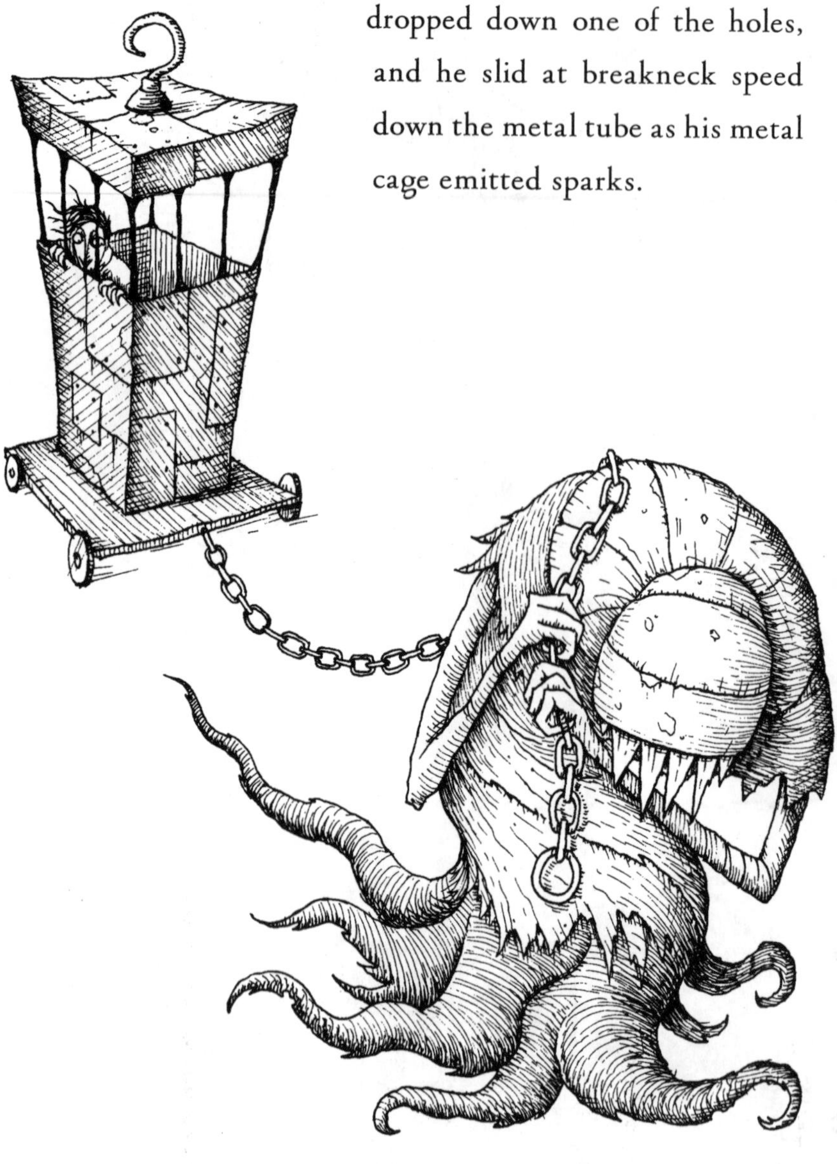

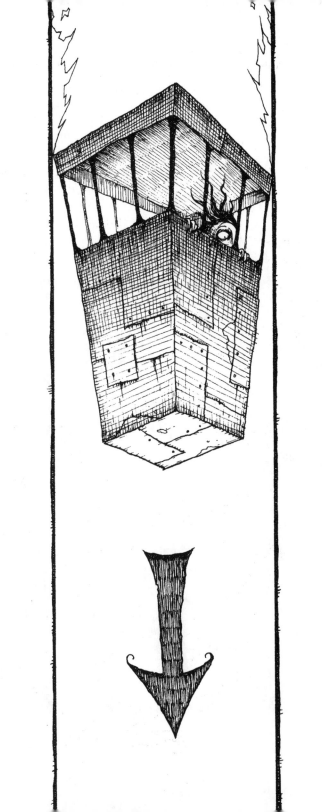

The cage hit the ground with a loud crash. Zazil found himself in a factory of some sort that was every bit as bleak as the one he used to work in. One of the Charnoks walked over to him, released him from the cage and immediately shackled him to a machine on an assembly line.

Great... I'm a factory worker even on another plane of existence, Zazil thought.

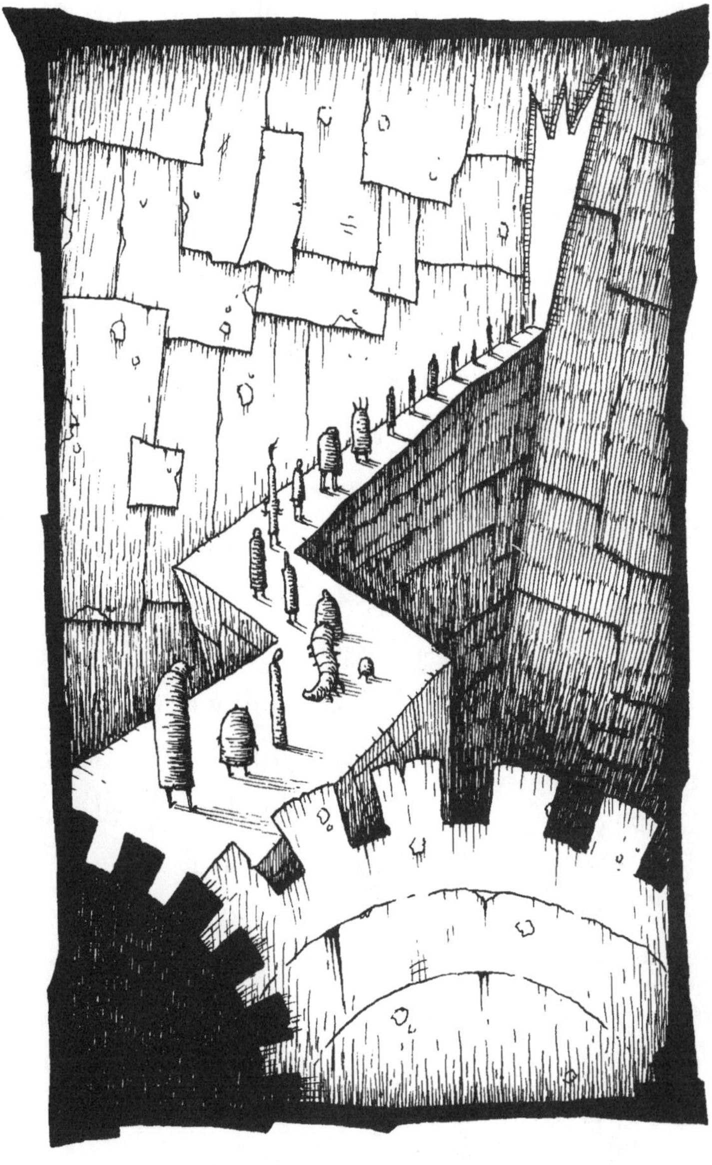

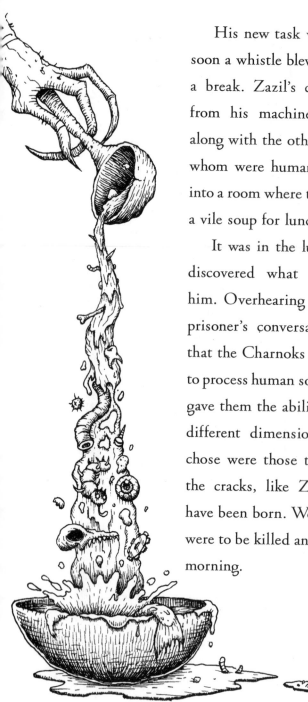

His new task was monotonous, but soon a whistle blew, and it was time for a break. Zazil's captors released him from his machine and prodded him along with the other prisoners, some of whom were human. They were all led into a room where they were to consume a vile soup for lunch.

It was in the lunchroom that Zazil discovered what was to become of him. Overhearing a few of the human prisoner's conversation, he discovered that the Charnoks had figured out how to process human souls into amulets that gave them the ability to travel between different dimensions. The souls they chose were those that slipped through the cracks, like Zazil, who shouldn't have been born. Worse yet, the humans were to be killed and processed the next morning.

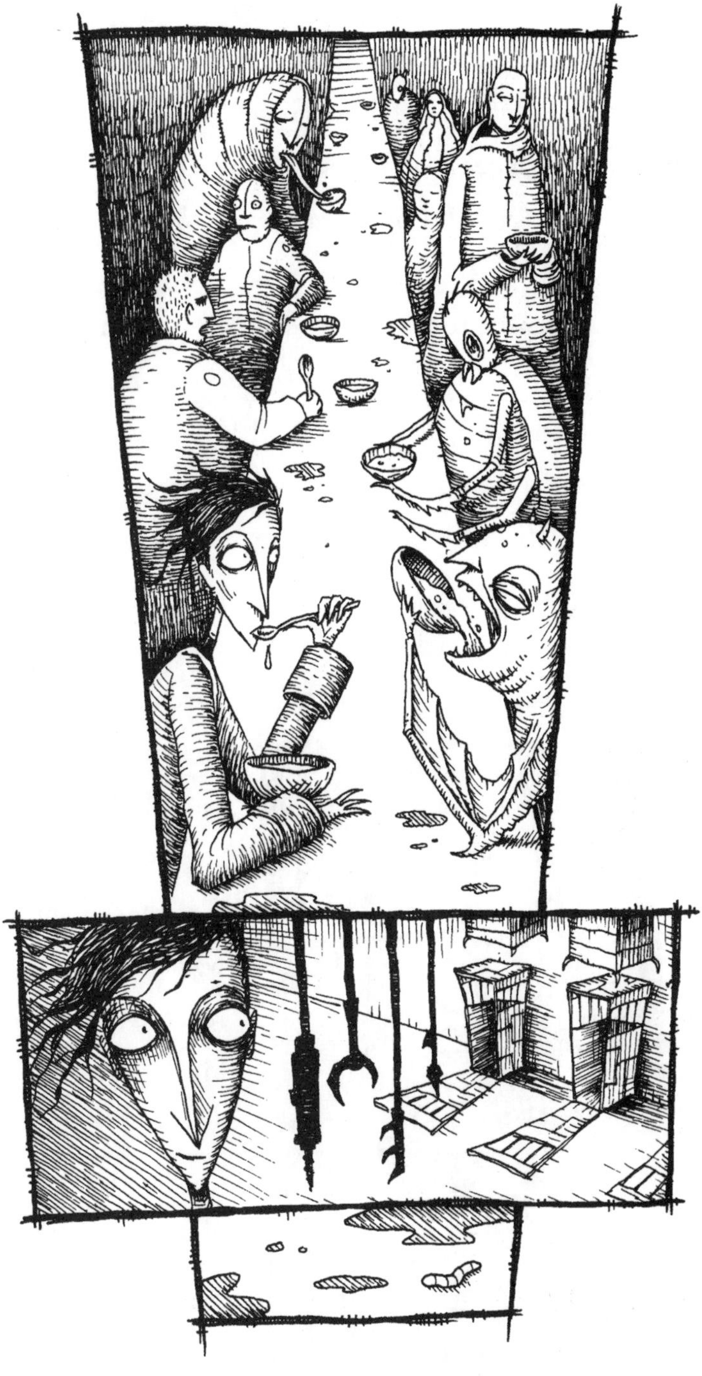

Once back at his workstation, Zazil developed a plan to escape. He figured that he didn't have much to lose. Waiting until the next shift showed up seemed like the best idea.

Perhaps I can get lost in the crowd and then crawl back up the tube I came out of. Once I'm back in the station I can try to get back on the train, he thought.

Shift One came to a close, and the next group of worker drones came marching down the corridor. Zazil fastened the clasps on his coat and prepared for escape. Just as he was doing so, the mask fell out and clattered on the floor. A Charnok noticed the racket and started on his way over to investigate.

In a panic, Zazil picked up the mask and put it on. This caused a curious effect. Almost immediately, Zazil became

covered in metal and blended into his surroundings, as if the mask knew he was in danger and reacted by disguising him. The Charnok walked right past him without seeing him and walked away, confused.

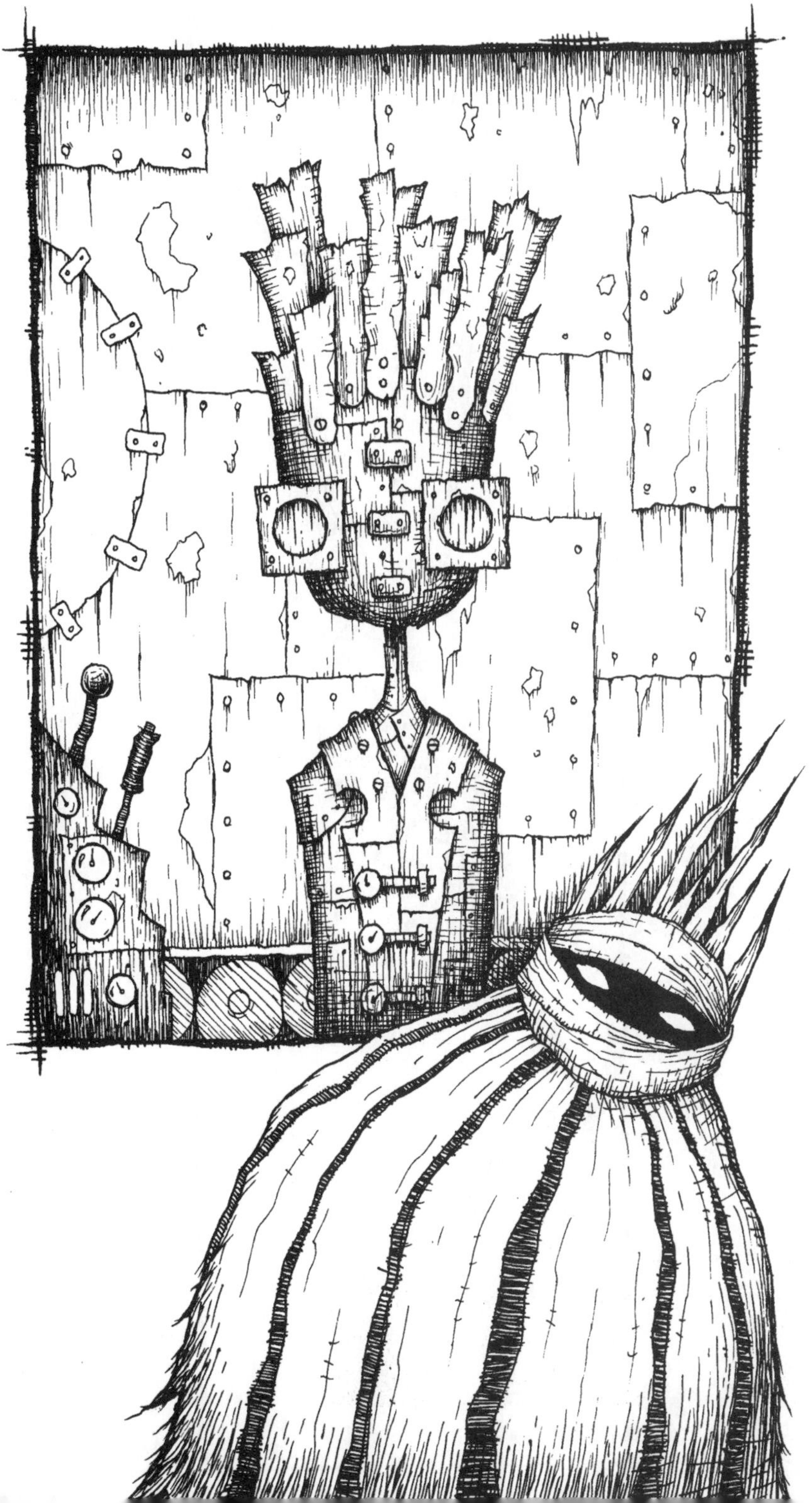

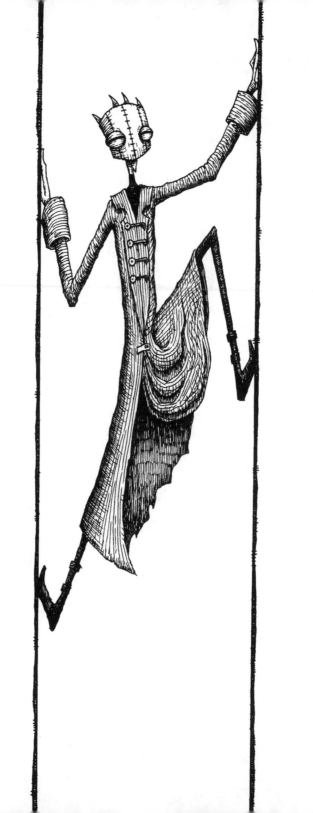

Waiting until it was safe, Zazil made his way up the tube. When he reached the top, he found no train station, just a large dark room with several holes in the rusted metal floor. Just when he thought all was lost, he remembered the amulet in his pocket. As he held it in the darkness, he recalled that the Charnok had used it for summoning the train. Soon he heard the same familiar sounds of steam and metal that he would hear while lying in bed at night. The train arrived and it was time to board once more....

This time, Zazil was alone on the train. As he sat staring at the amulet in his hand, he felt more tired than he had ever felt before. It was a deep, penetrating tiredness that he felt sleep couldn't even cure. He was tired of being chased. He was tired of working in factories, and he was tired of bad luck. It was at this time that he decided he would stay on the train until he found just the right place to stop.

Zazil rode the train for so long that he lost track of time. He passed through ancient abandoned cities, over monster-filled lakes, through gnarled mountains and a lonely, haunted forest. Just as he was starting to think he was safe, he heard garbled shouting in the car ahead of him. The Charnoks were looking for him. They had made the conductor stop the train in order to conduct a search.

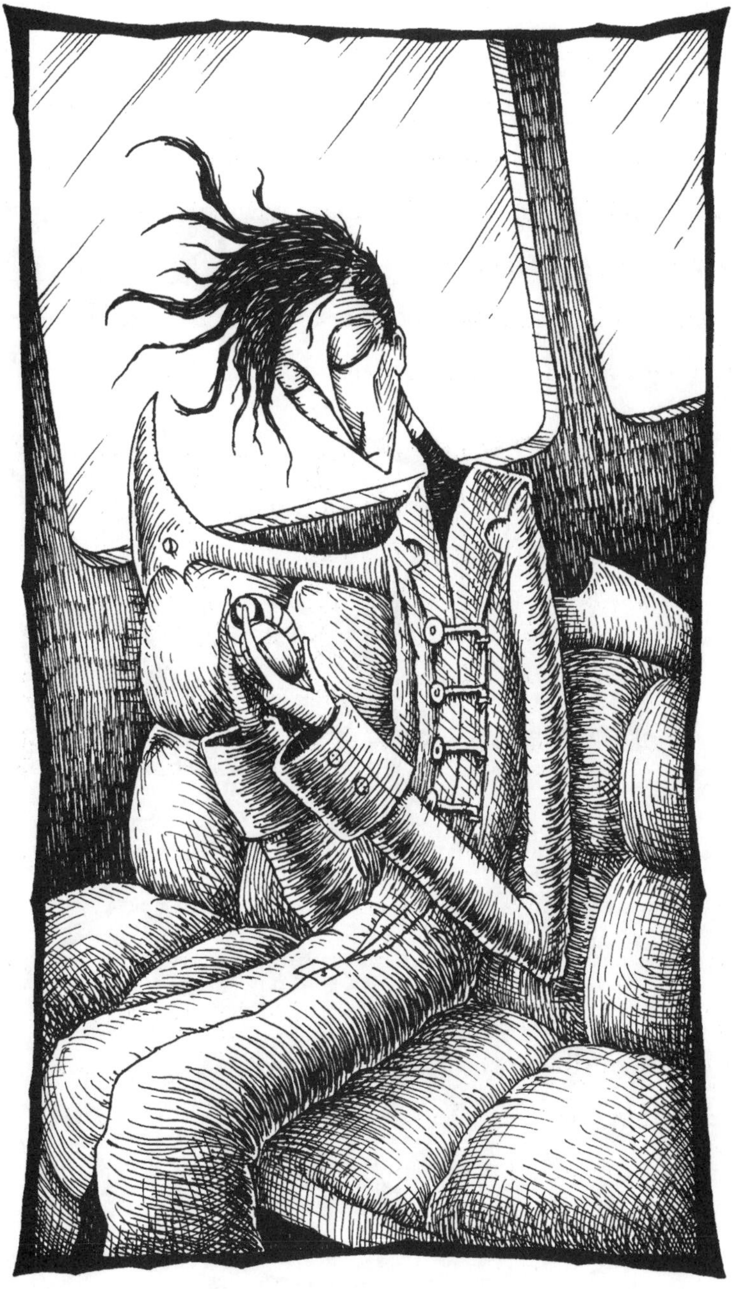

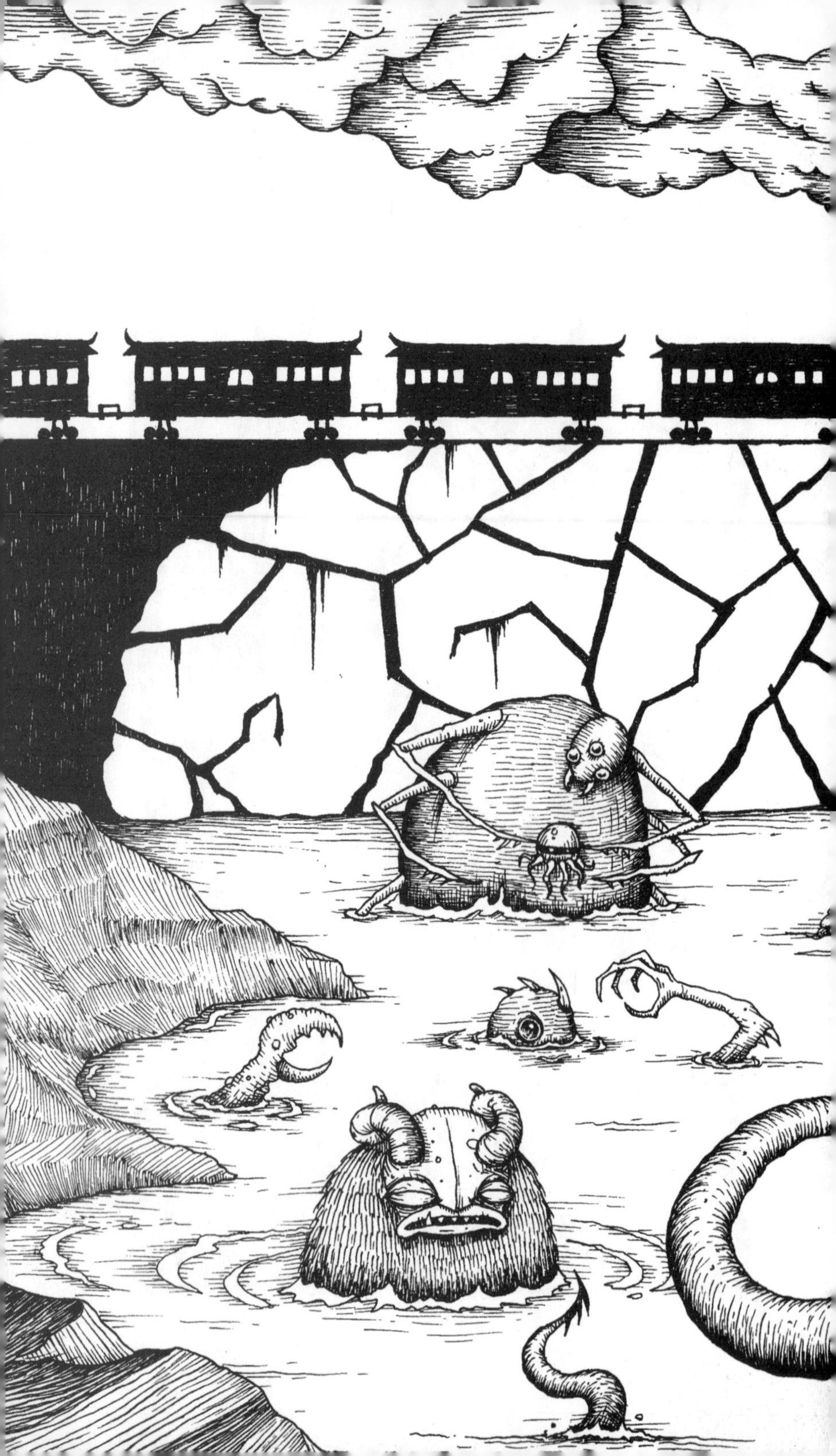

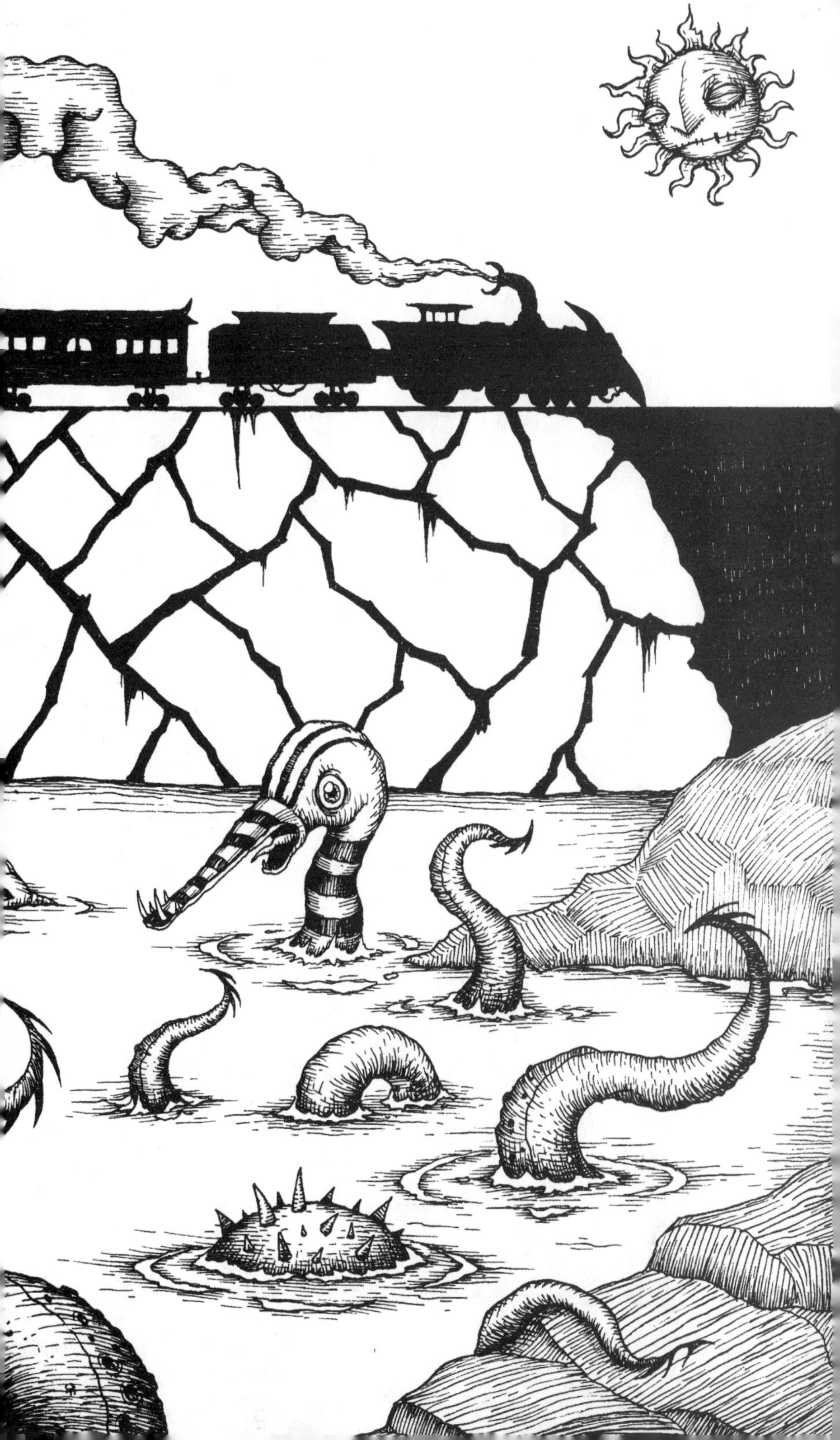

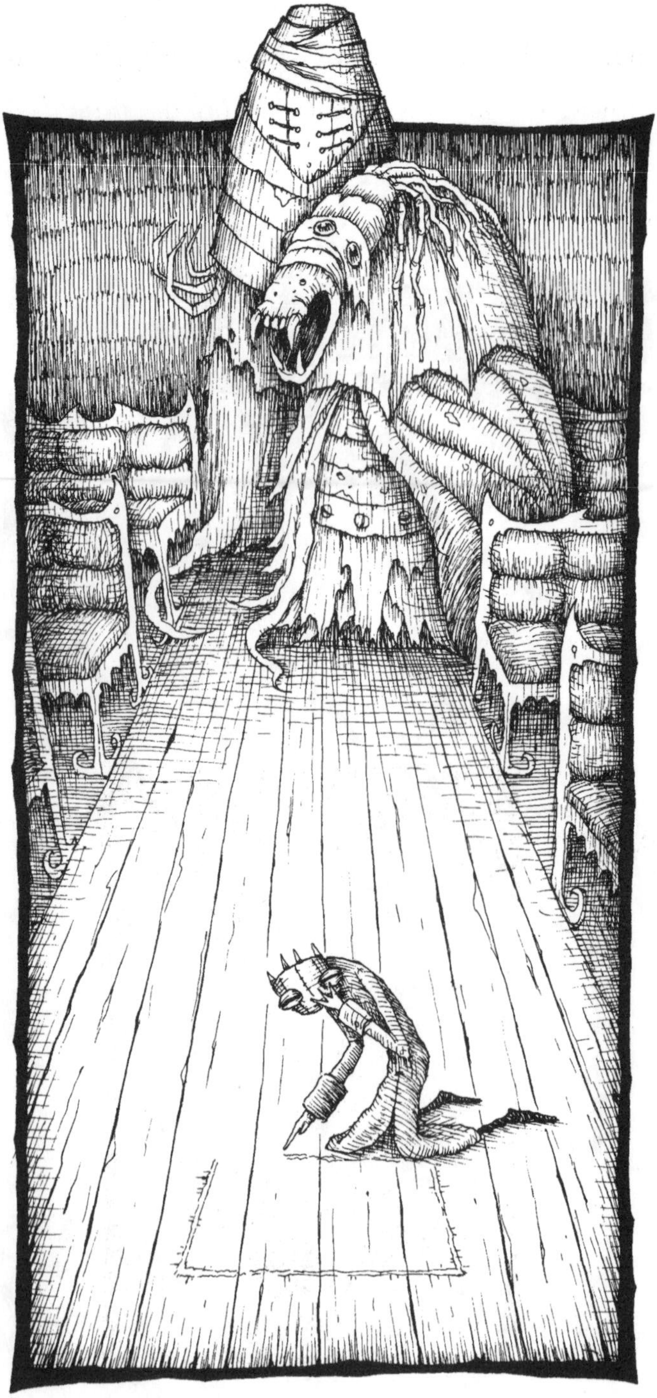

Knowing that the Charnoks would eventually find him, Zazil knew he had to somehow get off the train. Then he remembered what the sad Nog had shown him. Kneeling, he donned the mask. With his finger he traced a small rectangle in the dust on the floor. He then stood up and began to walk around it.

As he was performing the ritual, the door burst open. The Charnoks had found him! Just as one of them slashed its diamond-sharp claws at him, a stairway appeared on the floor. Zazil quickly ran down it. As he descended the stairs, the opening above him closed and he was left in the murk of a passage between worlds.

Zazil reached his hands out and felt walls on both sides of him. Stepping forward, he tripped as he discovered another set of stairs leading up. Carefully climbing them, he wondered what kind of hell he would find this time. Suddenly, he hit his head on something that felt like wood. He reached up and pushed on it. It was a door out!

Once Zazil was out of the passage, he surveyed his surroundings. *Nothing hostile here*, he thought after stepping up the stairs and onto a cobblestone-paved street in a narrow alleyway. He made his way down the alley and turned the corner to find a wider street lined with shops. First he passed a tailor's shop and then a bakery. Finally, he stopped at a clockmaker's shop and stood there observing the sign. He felt as if he'd been there before. At that moment, he realized he was in his home town...

Strangely, Zazil felt a sense of disappointment, as one might, having just returned to the same boring old town that he came from. It was more than that, though.... While he was on his journey, at least he had escaped from his monotonous, routine life. Being chased by monsters from Hell was at least more exciting than going to work. Now

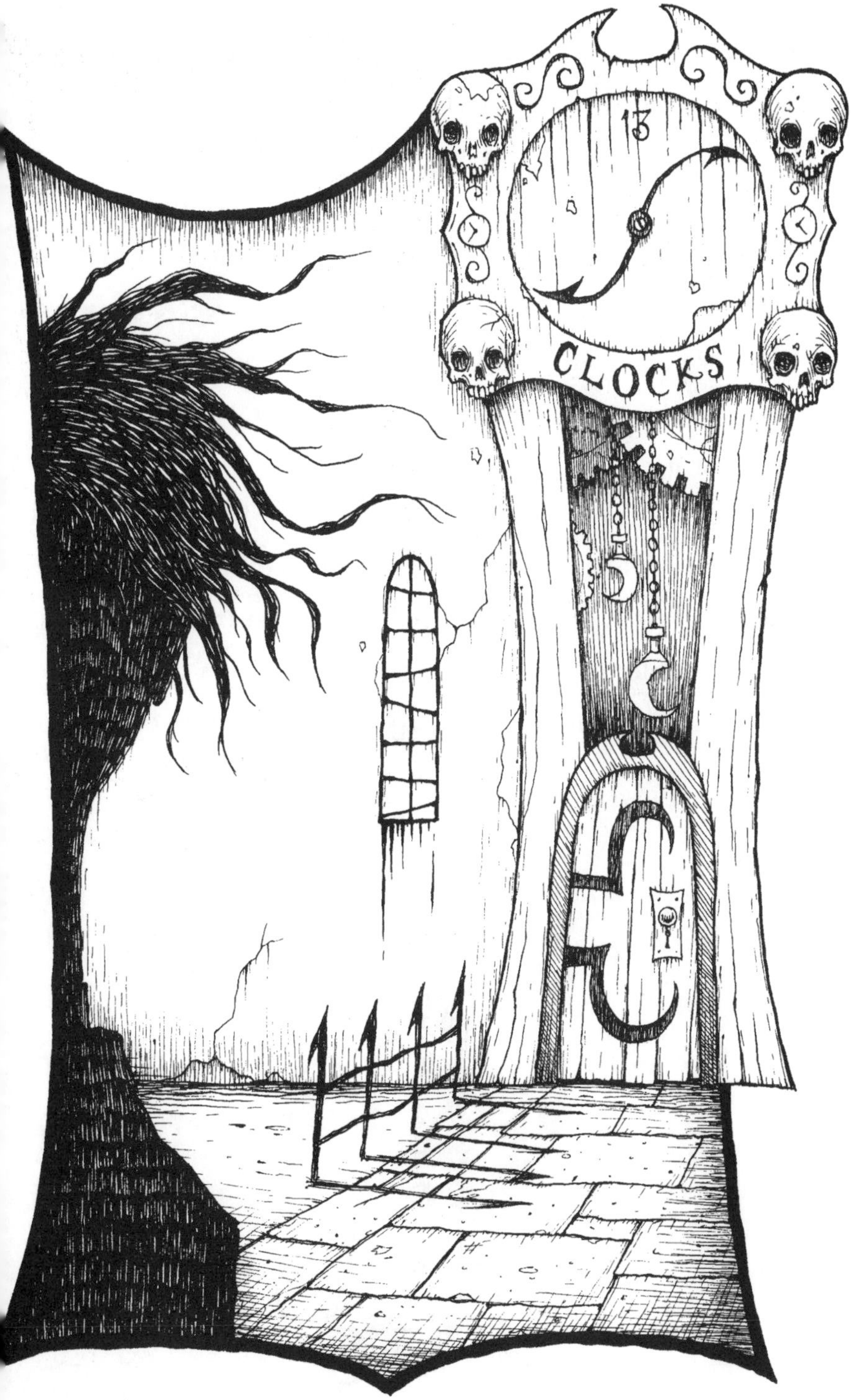
13
CLOCKS

that he was back, he would have to start all over. He'd have to find a new job and maybe even a new place to live. The crushing stress of reality began washing over him.

Zazil, deep in thought, continued his walk through town until he came to a street he had not seen since his mother died. He stopped, frozen, staring at the street sign. And then, for a reason he did not know, he began walking once more and kept on walking until he arrived at the house where he grew up.

That's strange, thought Zazil when he saw a warm, flickering light emanating from his old bedroom window. As far as he knew, no one had lived there for years. In fact, a lot of the people who lived in his neighborhood had moved due to the lack of jobs. When a huge, modern factory opened in the next city over, most of them had skipped town to work there.

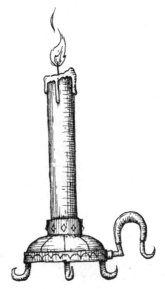

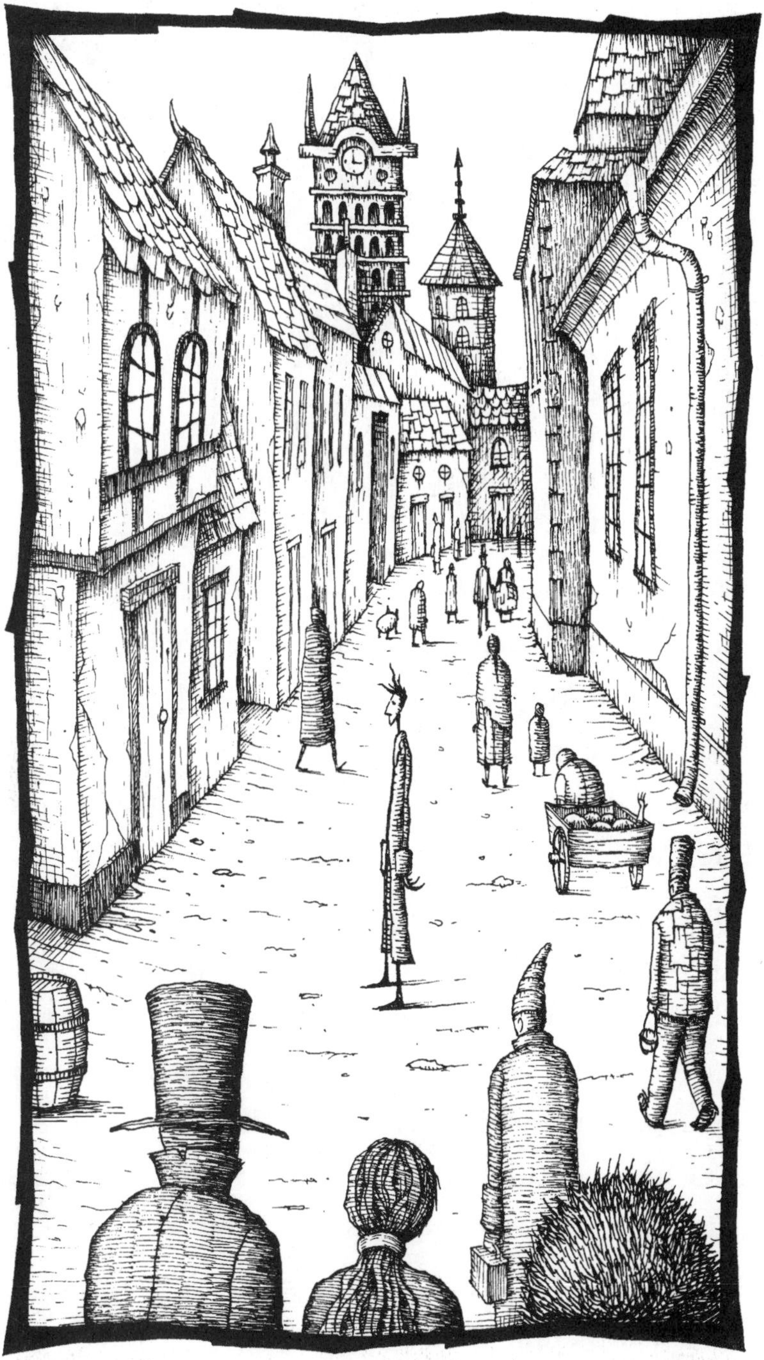

A sudden nostalgia swept over Zazil as he stood in front of his old house, and he had the urge to look inside just one more time. He knocked on the door, hoping the new tenants wouldn't mind if he had one last visit. As he knocked, the door creaked open. Politely, he called out "Anyone home?" There was no answer. Just as he was turning around to leave, he spied familiar furniture in the living room. Creepier yet, he saw a picture of him and his mother in a gilded frame.

This prompted him to enter. Once inside, he discovered that all of the things in the living room were just the same as when he had lived there as a child. Then he heard a voice coming from the hallway that made the wee hairs on his neck stand straight up. It was his mother.

Then it dawned on him. The Nog's magic had sent him back in time. A little spooked, Zazil forged ahead to his old bedroom.

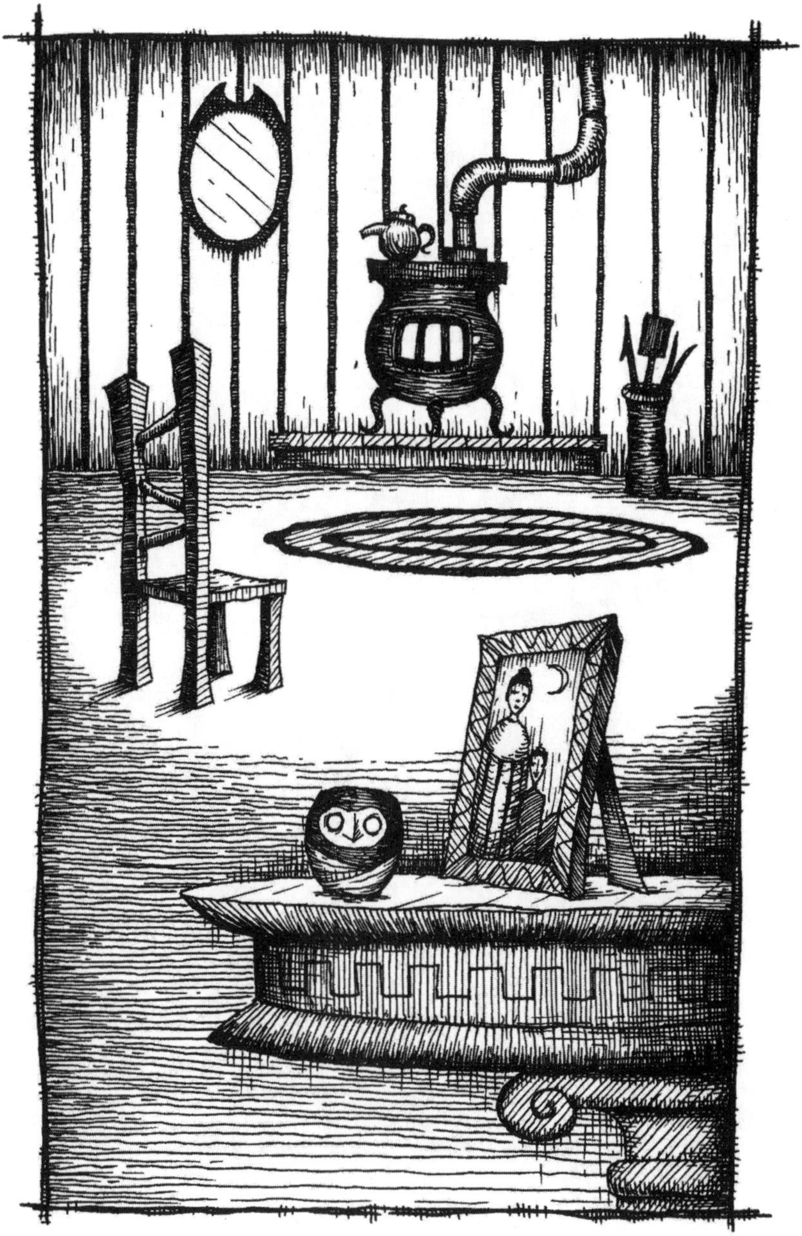

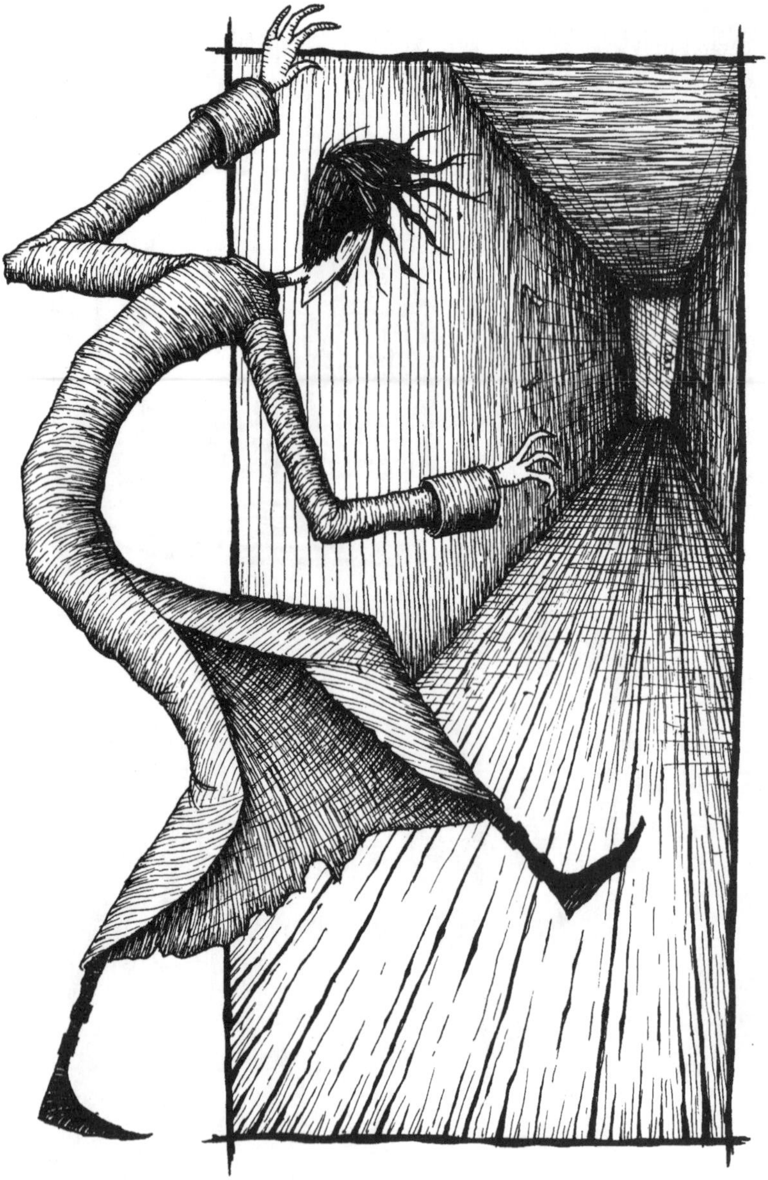

The hall leading to his old bedroom was dark, but it didn't deter Zazil from going down it. He heard voices again as he crept down the hall. He stopped when he reached his door, somewhat afraid of what he might find. Gathering up every last ounce of courage, he slowly opened the door. What he found shocked him. There, lying in the bed that he had once slept in was his 13-year-old self, talking to his mother for the last time.

Then as he realized what he was seeing, the 13-year-old Zazil saw him standing in the doorway. Their occupying the same place in time created a paradox, and they both began to vanish. All of Zazil's personal belongings began to disappear as well. It was beginning to appear as if he had never existed at all. During his last few moments of existence, he felt more relaxed and calm as he had ever felt. Zazil was finally at peace....

the End...